When Students Have
Time to Talk

WHEN STUDENTS HAVE TIME TO TALK

Creating Contexts for Learning Language

CURT DUDLEY-MARLING

DENNIS SEARLE

Faculty of Education
York University
Toronto, Canada

Heinemann
Portsmouth, NH

Heinemann
A division of Reed Elsevier Inc.

361 Hanover Street   Portsmouth, NH 03801-3959
Offices and agents throughout the world

Library of Congress Cataloging-in-Publication Data
Dudley-Marling, Curt.
   When students have time to talk : creating contexts for learning
language / Curt Dudley-Marling, Dennis Searle.
      p.   cm.
   Includes bibliographical references (p.).
   ISBN 0-435-08588-3
   1. Language arts (Elementary)—United States.   I. Searle, Dennis.
II. Title.
LB1576.D83   1991
372.6–dc20   91-12786
                                                        CIP

Designed by Wladislaw Finne.
Printed in the United States of America.
First printed 1991.
Printed on demand 1996.

Contents

vi
_____
Contents

Before We Get Started

A panel of scholars was asked to name humankind's greatest accomplishment. "That's easy," said the scientist, "our greatest accomplishment was putting a man on the moon." "No," insisted the physician, "the development of antibiotics is at least as great an achievement as putting a man on the moon, but has benefited far more people." The historian then shared her perspective that "the building of civilization is clearly our most significant achievement." "Yes," the linguist replied, "but none of these things would have been possible if we hadn't first learned language."

A moment's reflection reveals the beauty of language—its rich texture, its delicate rhythms and symmetry, and its subtle, but infinite, complexity. Even more impressive is its power. Language is the primary means by which we relate to each other, and it is our principal tool for thinking and problem solving. Language gives voice to the human spirit and sets us apart from the other animals. Arguably, language is our most precious inheritance and our greatest achievement.

Given the complexity of language, it's amazing that we learn it at all. But, in fact, we are so good at learning language that it's generally considered "child's play." Children begin tapping the power of language before their first birthday. And by the time they enter school, children use language as easily as adults, even if with less sophistication. But there is never a point in people's lives when they have mastered language. People continue to learn and grow as language users throughout their lives as they expand the range of purposes for which they use language and the physical and social settings in which they can fulfill those purposes. Children and adults also grow as they use language to represent their increasingly sophisticated understanding of the complex world in which they live.

Schools play an important role in children's language learning. Classrooms have the potential to be ideal language-learning environments because they can offer a range of things to talk about, reasons for talking, and audiences for talk. Formal and informal observations of classroom language indicate, however, that this potential is often unfulfilled.

We originally set out to write a book that would help teachers address the specific needs of language-delayed students by drawing on the language-learning potential of their classrooms. But as we wrote it became increasingly apparent that when teachers create rich language-learning environments they promote the language of all their students, not just those whose language is delayed. Since it seemed unnecessary to distinguish some students from others because of their abilities, our project evolved into this book, which teachers can use when working with all their students. In the pages that follow, we attempt to present a balance between language theory and practice in order to help teachers create and develop language-rich classrooms. We do not believe that rich language emerges in response to sure-fire activities for stimulating talk (for example, an oral language period from 9:00 to 9:30), but rather, through the development of a classroom culture in which students are immersed in language throughout the day and across the curriculum. It is important that students have opportunities to talk because:

- *When students have time to talk* they are able to try out their language, to listen to others respond to their language, and to hear other children and adults use language, getting the information they need to continue developing as language users.
- *When students have time to talk* they are challenged to stretch their linguistic resources even as they struggle to make sense in various physical and social settings.
- *When students have time to talk* teachers encourage them to draw on their background knowledge and experience to support school learning.
- *When students have time to talk* teachers learn about students' current state of language development and use this as a foundation on which to build.

• *When students have time to talk* teachers get a window on students' language development and the effect of their own instruction on students' learning. Wise teachers use these insights to plan and revise their instruction according to the individual needs of their students and to grow as teachers themselves—to learn to teach as they teach.

• *When students have time to talk* classrooms become places in which students and teachers get to know each other and live and learn together. Here teachers use talk to establish a diverse community of learners in which students collaborate, support, and celebrate each other's learning. In such an environment, classrooms become places for people.

We wish to thank all the teachers we've known who have taught us the value of talk in classrooms. We especially want to thank our families—our wives, Chris and Maija, for their love and support and for their comments on various drafts of this manuscript, and our children, Anne, Ian, Toni, and Tiina, for teaching us so much about language.

1

Learning Language at Home

Two-year-old Ian picks up a ball and bat, hands the bat to his father, and says, "Daddy, you hit. Me throw."

There is nothing remarkable about this utterance. It's the sort of thing any two-year-old might say. Yet in this "simple" five-word utterance, Ian has demonstrated a considerable understanding of the world and a remarkable facility with language. Amazingly, he has learned all this in a little over two years.

In just a few short years children learn how to use an unbelievably complex system—language—to understand and be understood in a wide range of settings. By the time they're four children may know as many as ten thousand words (Smith, 1986) and be able to demonstrate their knowledge of an astonishing number of rules for combining words into phrases and sentences. They know how and when to use language appropriately not only in a variety of settings but also with a range of audiences. And, of course, they never stop learning about language.

It's almost unimaginable that anyone, let alone a small child, could learn so much in such a brief time. Some language theorists in the 1960s tried to account for this extraordinary achievement by arguing that certain aspects of language were innate, that children were born "knowing" something about language. We now believe there is a simpler explanation for children's language learning: children learn language so quickly and easily because they are very good at learning and because parents typically provide nearly ideal conditions for language learning.

We can gain insight into language teaching and language learning by considering how children learn language naturally—before they come to school. We won't argue that the language-learning environment in the classroom should

1

precisely duplicate that in the home. It's not clear that this is desirable, even if it were possible. But some general principles of language learning are emerging from the study of normal language development, and these can inform classroom practice. So we begin by briefly reviewing why children learn language in the first place, what they learn about language that enables them to participate in a community of speakers, and how they learn all this in such a short time.

Why Children Learn Language

Nine-month-old Ian sits at the breakfast table and begins to cry. It's clear he wants something, but does he want more toast? More cereal? More milk? With each question Ian cries harder and ends up throwing his cereal on the floor. Finally, his mother asks if he wants some juice. He nods his head and stops crying. Less than a year later, under roughly the same conditions, Ian holds up his cup and says, "Juice, pease," and his father gets him some juice.

It's conventional wisdom that children learn language through such processes as imitation and reinforcement. Children presumably imitate the language they hear in their homes, and parents respond with lavish praise. Although imitation and praise no doubt have a role in language learning, most children, like Ian, learn language primarily because it works. And it is this discovery—that language is a powerful tool for getting things done—that sets children on the path of language learning.

Young children begin using language to obtain the goods ("more milk") and services ("horsey ride") they desire. Later, they learn to use language for a variety of additional purposes: interacting with others, describing, reporting, predicting, imagining, thinking and learning ("what's this called?"), and many others.

Although language will never again be learned as rapidly as it is during the first four or five years of life, people continue to learn how to use language to meet their needs throughout their lives. The motivation for learning language never changes: People learn language because it allows them to fulfill their needs. Language is a tool for getting things done.

What Children Learn About Language

But what do children learn about language that enables them to tap its power? As interested adults, we tend to focus on vocabulary. A child's first word is such a notable event that most of us can easily recall the first words spoken by our own children. Parents may celebrate these first words with a phone call to grandparents and even record a reenactment of the event with an audio or, in this increasingly electronic age, a video recorder. From this modest beginning children soon learn hundreds and then thousands of words to represent objects, actions, and events.

Although this achievement is in itself remarkable enough, children don't simply learn words. They learn ways of combining words into phrases and sentences to represent relationships between objects and events. The utterance "Ball floor" (meaning "The ball is on the floor"), for example, represents the objects "ball" and "floor" but, more importantly, it also indicates the physical relationship between the ball and the floor. In this case, the ball is *on* the floor. In addition, these word combinations can involve ordering rules (syntax) that represent meanings not present in the words themselves. The meaning of "Me eat cookie" ("I ate the cookie") is more than the sum of the meanings of *me + eat + cookie.* In this example, something has happened to the cookie, and the implication is that the cookie no longer exists—it's been eaten. As children get older they learn to represent increasingly complex kinds of relationships between objects and events—instrumental ("I eat with fork"), possessive ("My ball"), agent-object ("Me kick ball"), and so on (see Brown, 1973).

Children's knowledge of language forms, syntax, and vocabulary does not exist apart from their knowledge of the world. Language forms are essentially a code (Bloom and Lahey, 1978) by which we represent our world knowledge or our "theory of the world." So at the same time that children are learning the language code, they are also learning how the world works. Children learn that dogs bite but doors don't; children eat cookies but cookies don't eat children. Sometimes children's theories of the world are different from the worldview of adults. When Dennis Searle was a very small boy, he believed that the top half of toast was for girls (because it was round) and the bottom half for boys (because it was square), to the amusement of his family. But with experience, Dennis's understanding of the world, like that of all children, moved closer to that of the adults within his community.

During the first few years of their lives, gradually but certainly, children learn to use words and word-ordering rules to represent their enlarging experience and to fulfill an expanding variety of communicative intentions. But this isn't the whole story. If language use is more complicated than learning words and word-ordering rules, so is the challenge for the language learner. Children must also learn how to use language appropriately in conversational settings—what to say and how to say it in a range of social contexts. Children learn, for example, how the relative status of speakers and listeners affects politeness. "Give me some candy" might be an effective way to get a piece of candy from a friend but not from adults who prefer that children use a more polite form ("May I please have a piece of candy?"). Children also learn how shared background experience affects what they say and how they say it. They can reasonably describe a lost toy to their parents by recalling, "It's like the one I got for Christmas," but this strategy won't work very well with people outside the family. Children also learn that audience and setting affect word choice ("We use that word at home but not in church"). And they learn general "rules" about turn taking, staying on topic, being sufficiently explicit, repairing misunderstandings, and so on.

Children not only learn how to use various rules governing the use of language in conversational settings, they also learn that the deliberate violation of language conventions can have a particular meaning. A mother who walks into her ten-year-old son's room and announces, "It's ten o'clock," may seem to violate the conversational principle concerning relevance, since the time of day isn't at issue. But most children will have no trouble recognizing that this mother is gently letting her son know that it's time to go to bed.

Children learn rules governing the content, form, and use of language, but they do not learn these rules separately. Every language act simultaneously taps children's knowledge of the world, their knowledge of language forms, and their knowledge of how these various rules operate in actual conversational settings.

In addition, children's knowledge of the rules of language, like that of adults, is implicit. The explicit knowledge of language rules is not a necessary condition for language learning. In fact, from our perspective a precise description of the rules governing the form or use of language may not even be possible—there are too many complex, interacting factors that affect language use in actual conversational settings. We can illustrate this complexity with an example. Say you want something someone else has. How do you ask for it? Do you say, "Please may I have X?" or "Can I have X?" or "Give me X." It really depends, doesn't it? It depends on your audience. You might ask one way if you were talking to your spouse or a good friend and another way if you were talking to someone you hardly knew. And it wouldn't always do to opt for more polite forms, since their use might convey meanings you don't intend. The more polite "Would you please hand me the hammer?," for example, could be taken, in some contexts, to mean "I'm getting a little impatient with you" or to indicate coolness. And it's not just audience that affects the choice of politeness forms. Urgency would be another factor ("Call the hospital"). Setting is another. Even if you were talking to your best friend, the form of your request might be different if it were made in a church rather than in your basement, or on the golf course rather than during a corporate board meeting.

Clearly, language use is very complex. Yet despite its complexity, children do learn language. This is a tribute to their skill as learners.

How Children Learn About Language

IAN: Mommy, read book me.
MOMMY: Okay, Ian. Sit on the couch and I'll read you a book.

Children learn language because it works, but parents play an important role in ensuring that children's language does indeed work. In the above example, Ian's mother didn't respond to his request by praising him for producing such a good sentence ("Good talking, Ian"). Nor did she try to correct his grammar ("No, Ian. Say, 'Mommy, please read me the book' "). She did what almost any parent would have done—she read him the book.

Parents surround their children with language, talking to them or around them almost constantly. As Judith Lindfors (1987) phrases it, parents immerse their children in a "veritable language bath." This bath of language shows children how powerful language is and gives them the information they need to develop as language users.

Parents also give their children plenty of opportunities to use language. It's not unusual in many homes for everyone to stop and listen whenever a very young child speaks. As they get older, however, children have to learn to "fight" for the conversational floor just like everyone else. Learning how to get the floor is something else kids learn about language.

Parents provide opportunities for their children to hear and use language in a variety of authentic conversational milieus where all the factors (different settings, audiences, and so on) that affect language use are naturally present. But parents do not, in general, deliberately set out to teach their children language. In fact, the rare occasions when parents do try to teach language often result in amusing interactions such as this one:

ANNE: I pulled on my tooth and it bleeded.
MOTHER: It bled?
ANNE: Yeah. It bleeded.

That young children eventually learn conventional forms even though parents, despite what they may believe, rarely correct their children's language "errors," indicates that corrections do not play an important role in children's language development. Here is an illustrative example.

Two-year-old Toni and his father were walking to the park. Toni ran ahead to see who was at the park, then returned and said to his father, "Somebody not be here." His father replied, "I guess they must be at supper."

In this example, Toni made almost all the wrong decisions. He chose *somebody* instead of *no one, not be* instead of *is,* and *here* instead of *there.* But Toni's father, like most parents, responded to his son's intentions ("I guess they must be at supper"), not to the form of his language. Yet at sixteen Toni makes all the right decisions even though his father didn't correct his "errors" when he was young.

What can we learn from the kind of language-learning environments parents provide for their children? The focus of the language interactions between parents and their children is on communication. Parents rarely try to *teach* language. The "language lessons" they provide are lessons only in retrospect. Instead, parents use language to understand and be understood by their children. They listen to what their children have to say and treat what they have to say as meaningful. In communicating with their sons and daughters, parents provide the information their children need to learn what language is for and how to use it. Certainly difficulties sometimes arise, but when there are problems with the language-learning environments that parents provide, it's usually because parents stop trying to communicate with their children, perhaps because they lose faith in children's ability to learn language.

It's also worth noting what *cannot* be learned from studying the verbal interactions between parents and children, and that is: Precisely what do parents do to encourage language development? No isolated language-teaching strategies are emerging in the literature on the language between parents and children. In fact, studies of parental language input interactions with young children in cultures around the world demonstrate that there are few, if any, universals, although most parents seem to trust that their children *will* learn to talk and typically provide them with frequent opportunities to hear and use language in authentic conversational settings.

Children learn language because it works. But to get it to work they need to learn a system of rules for representing objects and events and how to use these rules appropriately. This kind of learning is very complex and can't be reduced to a collection of discrete, isolated rules. Children don't experience the world and *then* learn word-ordering rules and vocabulary, and how language works in social contexts. Rather, they discover how these various language systems interact as they learn what to say and how to say it to fulfill a variety of purposes in a range of contexts. And they do this by being regularly exposed to language in authentic communicative settings in which all the factors that affect language use are naturally present.

2 *Learning Language in School*

Learning to speak effectively may be the most important skill students can acquire—even more important than learning to read or write (Jones, 1988). Students' skill in using language will affect how well they can participate in almost every facet of the academic and social life of the classroom. And, while it will be difficult for them to get along in adulthood if they can't read or write, it will be virtually impossible for them to succeed if they can't speak effectively. Therefore, oral language development must be an important goal for all teachers.

In the previous chapter we gave a general overview of children's language learning before they come to school. In general, children learn language quickly and easily because of their own remarkable language-learning abilities and because parents usually provide nearly ideal conditions for learning language. Although teachers can't reproduce the conditions for language learning found in children's homes, they should be mindful of some general principles of language teaching and language learning that derive from our knowledge of how and why preschool children learn language and what they learn about language.

In this chapter we present six global language-learning principles that we believe provide the foundation for the development of rich language-learning environments in our classrooms. These principles, which we will continue to discuss and develop throughout this book, will provide the basis for more specific discussions of language teaching in subsequent chapters.

Don't Fragment Language

William Hull, a colleague of John Holt, observed, "If we taught children to speak they'd never learn" (quoted in Holt,

1982). Hull didn't mean that teachers are incapable of helping children learn language but that too often when we deliberately try to teach children, we break learning into bits and pieces. This approach deprives learners of personal motivation, since learning isolated skills fulfills no purpose beyond earning the teacher's praise.

The process of fragmenting language for instructional purposes is based on the assumption that language is indeed fragmentable, that the sum of the pieces (language skills) equals the whole (language). But language skills are neither discrete nor independent. And learning language skills (such as vocabulary and word-ordering rules) in isolation bears little resemblance to what language users do when they use these skills in real-world communicative settings. As Edelsky states, language systems "not only operate in context; they also are interdependent, each one having consequences for the other. In any instance of genuine oral or written language use, a choice in one system has ramifications for what choices or interpretations are possible in another" (1984, 9).

Learning to talk is analogous to learning to ride a bicycle. Bicyclists use a number of identifiable skills in the process of getting from one place to another. They balance, pedal, steer, monitor traffic conditions, and so on. One might be tempted to teach children to ride by teaching these various skills one by one. But—and here's the problem—bicyclists don't simply balance. They balance and simultaneously steer, pedal, and watch traffic. And of course, bicyclists who just try to balance without also steering and pedaling will certainly fall over. Balancing by itself only superficially resembles what bicyclists actually do when they ride a bicycle.

Similarly, people don't just say isolated words or order words in random sentences. Language users express themselves in meaningful ways in a variety of situations, each of which demands different things of their linguistic and cognitive abilities. They use language in contexts where they must simultaneously orchestrate all they know about language and all they know about the world. And unlike the bicyclist, whose task doesn't change much from one time to the next, language users must constantly adjust their use of various language systems according to the requirements of different audiences, different purposes, and different physical settings.

Provide Authentic Situations for Using Language

Language must be learned in authentic settings in which real speakers and listeners try to fulfill their intentions and transact meaning. Children can only learn how language works by actually using language themselves and hearing it used by others in real-life settings. In contrived settings, like those designed deliberately and explicitly to teach language, children learn how to use language only in similar contexts, which they are unlikely to encounter outside of the the language lesson. Although children can learn fragmented bits and pieces of language taught in isolation, that's all they'll learn—fragmented bit and pieces. Real language learning depends upon experiencing the power of language in all its richness and complexity in settings where real speakers and listeners work together to get something done.

Let Students Try Language Out

Children learn language by actively trying it out and only gradually gaining control over its use. When Anne was three she spent a week in Charlottesville, Virginia, with her parents and her dog. Perhaps out of boredom, Anne began teasing the dog mercilessly. Her father scolded her and asked her to "stop harassing the dog." Anne asked what *harassing* meant, and her father told her it meant that she was "bugging" the dog. Later that same day Anne asked to go swimming and her father said she couldn't. This prompted Anne to run to her mother crying, "Mommy, Mommy, Daddy's harassing me."

Anne tried out *harass* because it seemed to her to be a potentially useful word. It didn't matter that *harass* is a sophisticated word. Lots of kids use words like this if they find them useful. And it didn't matter that Anne didn't quite get the adult meaning of *harass*. By using the word she tested its meaning and, in time, she would gain control over it. Three years later Anne suggested to her father that he get the dog out from under his desk by "harassing it." This is still slightly different from the adult meaning of the word but it's much closer than it had been three years earlier.

Similarly, when Ian's grandmother visited his preschool she asked him to take her around his classroom and tell him the names of various objects. When they returned home Ian took his grandmother around the house labeling household objects (table, chair, lamp . . .) for her since this was, presumably, the kind of stuff grandmothers wanted to know about.

Experimentation with language isn't limited to preschool children. All children, and even adults, experiment with language in order to make sense of it. Only by trying language out in various physical and social settings do we gain control over its power as a tool for getting things done.

Let Students Experiment with Language

This is a corollary of the previous principle. Children learn language by trying it out, but they will be much more willing to try out language if they can do so without risk.

Piaget taught us that children learn by *taking chances.* Classrooms should provide students with an environment in which they are free to take risks. Often we fear that if we don't tell children that they have misused a word or a language form they won't learn the "correct" form. This isn't so. If Anne's father had corrected her misuse of *harass,* he may only have succeeded in discouraging her from experimenting with language in the future and by so doing, interfered with her language development.

Teachers' corrections can have the same effect on students' language. If Timmy's teacher responds to his news, "My dad and me goed to the Blue Jays' game yesterday," by saying, "Who won?" she affirms that it's *what* Timmy has to say that's important to her and not *how* he says it. If, conversely, she responds, "Can you say 'My dad and *I went* to the Blue Jays' game'?" she indicates that she cares more about the form of what he says. In this case, Timmy may feel reluctant to share news with his teacher again. In the worst case, corrective feedback may discourage some children from talking in school at all.

Trust Students' Ability to Learn

One reason teachers sometimes correct students' language use and try to teach language explicitly is that they may have lost faith in a particular student's ability to learn like other children. Consider the following example, in which a teacher interacts with Miles, a student who frequently struggled in school. Miles is explaining a picture:

TEACHER: What are you doing in the picture?

MILES: Skating.

TEACHER: Will you tell me a sentence about it?

MILES: I go skating.

TEACHER: Where?

MILES: In the Mill Pond.

TEACHER: In the Mill Pond? Are you right in the pond?

MILES: Yeah. No.

TEACHER: No. [*Laughs*] Where are you?

MILES: Skating.

TEACHER: Yes, but you're not in the Mill Pond. You'd be all wet if you were in it. Where are you?

MILES: Skating, I think. I don't know. Icing, I think.

TEACHER: Sometimes we say, "Skating *at* the Mill Pond."

MILES: Yeah.

In our experience this is not a particularly unusual example. The teacher posits an improbable meaning (that Miles was skating *in* the pond) in part because she believes that Miles was insufficiently explicit. Her response seemed to confound Miles, who became increasingly confused about what she wanted from him ("Skating, I think. I don't know. Icing, I think").

These kinds of interactions result, we believe, when teachers doubt children's language abilities and lose faith in children's capacity to learn without their explicit help. We doubt very much if the teacher would even have noticed if a speaker she judged to be more competent stated that he had been skating "in" the pond. But here, the teacher's lack of trust in the child's ability seemed to influence her to respond in a way that, from Miles's perspective at least, results in nonsense.

Considering how children learned about language and the world before they came to school, there is every reason to trust in children's ability to learn in school. It's not the case that any child, even if he or she may struggle, *doesn't* or *can't* learn. Some children may not have learned as much as their peers, or they may not be learning what *we* want them to learn. Again, we must believe in their marvelous linguistic and cognitive abilities. Trusting that students are able to learn will not guarantee learning, but losing faith in them may ensure their failure.

Create Challenging Situations

Children learn language because it works, because it fulfills their personal needs. We can't give our students language, nor can we give them reasons for using language. Those responsibilities rest primarily with them. But we can promote language learning by creating or exploiting situations that challenge students to expand their linguistic resources. We can, for example, encourage students to use language for different purposes by placing them in a variety of situations deliberately chosen for their potential to encourage different language functions and forms. A construction activity with blocks may, for example, encourage the use of language for forward planning. Sharing times may encourage reporting or describing. Or a teacher may help a student to become more explicit by encouraging her to participate in dialogues that require explicitness, as in this example (from Strickland et al., 1989):

NEETA: This is my favorite part, but not the funniest. He puts it on the bed.
KATRINAH: What is "it"?
NEETA: Put it on . . .
KATRINAH: What is "it"? I don't understand what "it" is.
BAHAR: [What] you're talking about . . . what's that red thing? You say it.
NEETA: Yeh.
NEETA: She [*referring to an earlier discussion*] just said it. A cat ring.
KATRINAH: Then why don't you say that instead of just saying "it," "it," "it." (198)

Teachers may be able to stimulate language development by manipulating a variety of environmental factors—like audience and physical setting—that can affect talk. But unless children have real reasons for wanting to communicate and unless they experience the richness and power of language in many different kinds of settings, their language will not flourish.

Children learn language by talking and by hearing other people talk. Classrooms that discourage talk will never be good places for language learning. But teachers who engage in genuine conversation with their students and who encourage them to talk with each other provide the most favorable conditions for language learning. Roger Brown's advice to parents is good advice for teachers, too.

Believe that your child can understand more than he or she can say, and seek, above all to communicate. To understand and be understood. To keep your minds fixed on the same target. In doing that, you will, without thinking about it, make 100 or maybe 1,000 alterations in your speech and action. Do not try to practice them as such. There is no set of rules of how to talk to a child that can even approach what you unconsciously know. *If you concentrate on communicating, everything else will follow.* (1977, 26, emphasis added)

3 Creating Environments for Learning Language

The view of language learning we have been presenting certainly downplays the role of the teacher as instructor. From this perspective language cannot be taught in the traditional sense. Teachers cannot *tell* students how to use language. So what is the role of the teacher? Are teachers relegated to the role of passive observers while students do all the work? Or is it enough simply to take advantage of situations that occur fortuitously during the day? The answer to both these questions is no. An effective language teacher consciously immerses students in language, taking care to expose them to different kinds of settings, and challenging them to tap their linguistic resources. As Jones (1988) states:

> One learns language by being in a situation that calls language forth. So we should take the focus away from language teaching and on to language learning. The teacher's job is to provide those rich and varied contexts that will enable the language to grow. (14)

In this and following chapters we will try to help teachers create environments that challenge students to discover the power of language to meet some of the social, emotional, and cognitive demands of their lives in and out of school.

Consider the Emotional Setting

Before we consider the physical characteristics of a good environment for talk we need to consider the emotional and social environment. Even if the physical environment encourages talk, it can still be a risky business for many students. Students whose speech or language is immature risk ridicule by their classmates and possible correction by their teachers. If we want to encourage students to try out language we must provide an environment where they feel safe enough to experiment. They must feel that what they say and how they say it will be respected, and not subjected to ridicule or judgment. If students don't feel comfortable trying out new words or new ways of putting sentences together, their language development will be impeded, perhaps exacerbating problems they already have.

Teachers need to work to establish a classroom climate of trust and respect. Sometimes they may actively have to encourage students to respect the language of their peers. The most important influence here is the teacher's role as model. Teachers who listen respectfully to students when they speak and respond to what they have to say will provide a useful model for their students. But if teachers routinely evaluate their students' language, so will students. Or if teachers devalue dialect or nonstandard speech, and, by inference, dialect and nonstandard speakers, so will students.

It may also be necessary to develop classroom rules that promote respect for one another and support effective group work. The opportunity to discuss effective interaction together and develop rules is itself a valuable language activity. One teacher we know provides her class with one rule, "No unkindness!" which she insists all class members, including herself, observe. She then encourages students to work out more specific rules about behavior and interaction. Another teacher follows his first few group activities with discussions about "things that make groups work" and "things that prevent groups from working." The class then prepares a list of approved and prohibited kinds of behavior, which they periodically return to and amend throughout the year. These activities assure students of the teacher's confidence in them. They have worthwhile things to say and they will have the opportunity to speak out.

Create a Physical Setting for Talk

If we wish to immerse students in language we need to create physical environments that allow students to talk with and listen to their teachers, peers, and, if possible, other adults. The physical environment of the classroom can make interaction among students easy and give them lots to talk about.

*Create a Physical
Setting for Talk*

Sometimes classrooms are deliberately arranged in ways that discourage talk. Lining desks up in rows, for example, has a dampening effect even among college students. The practice of physically isolating "distractible" students from the rest of the class may prevent some students from talking at all.

Sometimes it is appropriate to provide students with quiet places for solitary work. But if we're serious about promoting language learning we must also organize classrooms to ensure that group work—communication, cooperation, and collaboration—also has a place. In many primary classrooms, for example, desks have been replaced with round or rectangular tables. In others, desks are arranged in clusters of three or four, allowing students to talk to each other easily. Some classrooms retain the traditional arrangement of desks in rows but also provide tables where students can work in groups and conversational areas where the class can gather for large-group discussions. In others, desks are in rows for quiet work, but students can rearrange them for the group work that is part of each day. All of these arrangements permit students to face each other, thereby inviting and encouraging sharing and cooperation.

Teachers can also promote talk in their classrooms by providing lots to talk about. Many classrooms contain activity centers with pet gerbils, fish tanks, nature displays, and so on. Students are encouraged to talk with each other if they are given the opportunity to visit these centers several students at a time and if the activities require or encourage interaction.

Teachers who regularly bring special objects and materials into the classroom will find that this practice encourages students to do the same. One eighth-grade teacher we know filled her classroom with souvenirs from her Caribbean vacation. Soon, many of her students, some of whom had moved to Toronto from the Caribbean, began bringing in their own Caribbean artifacts. These exhibits stimulated both formal and informal classroom discussions. Classroom exhibits such as these invite students to share, explain, question, and react. They may also inspire wide-ranging curriculum units. Such displays, however, should be refreshed regularly. As materials become familiar and their novelty wears off, they gradually lose their power to stimulate talk.

The presence of meaningful print in the classroom will also encourage students to talk and thus promote language development. A special education classroom we know displays daily and monthly schedules, biographical sketches of the students, children's poetry copied onto large pieces of tagboard and illustrated, sign-up sheets, children's written work, and book posters. There is a large collection of books for reading and comfortable places to read them in. Teachers and students regularly write notes to each other and then post them on a bulletin board. The presence of all this print invites reading, of course, but it also encourages students to discuss what's been written, perhaps helping each other to read the print in the environment around them.

In general, there is a strong reciprocal relationship between oral and written language. Reading, writing, speaking, and listening are inextricably linked, developing together, each supporting the other. Writers use talk to develop their topics, clarify their thinking, and discuss their writing with potential audiences. Readers use talk to consider what they will or have read. They also use talk as a means of sharing what they've read and extending their comprehension. Written language is an important source of data about oral language. Readers learn about words, about formal structures like passive tense, and about narrative structures by reading. So what our students learn about talk will affect their reading and writing. And what they learn about print will influence their oral language development. A language-rich classroom encourages all modes of language.

The nature of classroom activities will also affect the quantity and quality of student talk. The following two examples involve pairs of students working with two different computer programs. In the first, two girls, ages ten and eleven, work together on a drill-and-practice "problem-solving" program, for which there is only one correct answer (after a series of visual clues the user indicates whether the object is a "Gribbit" or a "Bibbit"). The girls take turns with the keyboard.

MARY: Short. He's fat. Red. He's definitely a Gribbit. [*Indicates her choices by hitting single keys*]
ROSE: My turn. Tall. Fat. Blue. And he's a Bibbit.
MARY: Yeah.

ROSE: One more time. [*Selects the same "game" again*]
   Your turn.
MARY: Tall. He's fat. He's red.
ROSE: He's a Bibbit.
MARY: He's a Bibbit.
ROSE: Are we going to do this again?
MARY: [*As she selects a different "game"*] No.
ROSE: I get to do this one, right?
MARY: Yes.

The talk proceeds in a similar manner for ten more minutes.
As we review this transcript, it is clear that the language is
vapid, characterized by a minimum of conversational interaction. Most of the talk is self-directing and requires no audience. In general, this closed-ended activity generates little
talk because there is little to talk about.

   In the second example, two third-grade students use a
computer program that enables them to draw graphics with
color. The students are free to draw whatever they wish.
The comparative openness of the task contributes to more
purposeful, extended talk.

JAN: Now what do you want to do?
TOM: I don't know.
JAN: Do you want to start all over?
TOM: Press "C." [*Instructions to the computer*] "C." Do "C."
   There.
JAN: What do you want to do?
TOM: It's my turn.
JAN: What do you want to do?
TOM: Something interesting. [*Referring to what they might
   "draw"*] A bunch of lines.
JAN: Cherries.
TOM: Cherries.
JAN: Yeah, cherries. Two cherries.
TOM: Two cherries. Big deal.
JAN: No? Then what're we going to do?
TOM: Okay. A Smurf.
JAN: Go ahead.
TOM: Change color.
JAN: Do you know how to draw a Smurf?
   [*At this point the students are engaged in the social*

*activity of working out turn taking and building a work
relationship.*]

TOM: Yeah, sure. Change the color. Forward . . . Miss [*calling
for the teacher; he consults with the teacher*]. This is
[*inaudible*].

JAN: I changed the background color.

TOM: Change it to a different color. Change it to white.

JAN: Okay.

TOM: A Smurf is blue. Here.

JAN: Okay. Wait. Let me finish.

TOM: Press [*inaudible*].

JAN: No, it doesn't.

TOM: It gets faster after [*voice trails off*].

JAN: But first we have to draw the Smurf's thing to be the
background [*inaudible*].

TOM: No. Because the Smurf is blue and it's exactly that
blue.

JAN: I know. But first we have to draw the background, don't
you? I mean, the Smurf first and the background doesn't
run into the Smurf.

[*Here the students use language to explain, develop
sequence, and provide rationale for their actions. They
then go on to work together to make sense of the computer instructions in order to work on their picture.*]

TOM: Okay. Press, do a white. No, the smurf wears a white
hat. Purple, do purple. Change color. [*Computer instructions*]

JAN: Shift. Change color.

TOM: Now what? Paint?

JAN: Yeah, paint. You have to draw a line all on the outside.

TOM: Yeah. We'll just make a box. Pen up. Now we'll change
the color to blue. How do we know which is blue?

JAN: [*Pointing to the keyboard*] This is white. This is blue.

TOM: Are you sure?

JAN: Yeah.

In this example there is a natural give-and-take to the talk
as the two students use language to negotiate, collaborate,
question, and direct. It's worth noting that over a period of
sixty minutes several groups of students were taped as they
worked with this program. During this time there wasn't a
single off-task utterance by any of the students. Given some
measure of control and an activity that captured their inter-

est, students had no difficulty confining their discussions to the task at hand.

This illustrates an important point. Rearranging classroom furniture and placing students in groups will not by itself generate quality talk. Students still need things that are interesting to them to talk about. And if the physical environment fails to generate talk, we need to reexamine the potential of the environment to stimulate language, not just the potential of the students to use language.

We don't wish to suggest that the environment operates independently of the teacher. Indeed, the talk that emerges provides opportunities for teachers to engage with students, helping them to extend their understanding and their language. In the following example, grade-ten students were working in a laboratory charting the passage of light through prisms. The presence of manipulative material encouraged playful experimentation and led to the following exchange between teacher and student:

LARRY: Hmm—that's funny.
ALLAN: What's funny?
LARRY: Want to see something funny?
ALLAN: Oh, what's going on inside?
LARRY: Mr. Potter . . .
TEACHER: Yes?
LARRY: What kind of refraction do you call that?
TEACHER: Well, if this comes here, what you're doing is splitting the beam, aren't you?
BRIAN: Yeah.
TEACHER: It hits that point and it just goes off in both directions at the same angle. And if that hits at sixty and that's a sixty-sixty-sixty, it looks like an equilateral triangle and everything's going to be the same and equal.

The conversation starts very simply. The boys are playing with the apparatus and produce an unusual effect when they direct the light onto the point of the prism. Having the equipment available allows the boys to experiment and hypothesize about their play. Then they involve the teacher, who starts by offering them the simple explanation they seek. The boys engage the teacher further by disagreeing with him.

LARRY: No.
TEACHER: What do you mean, no?

LARRY: It's not all the same.

TEACHER: Oh, I think those are probably coming out at the same angles. What you're doing is splitting this right on there. What happens when you do this? [*Turns the prism to adjust the angle at which light enters the prism.*]

LARRY: Bend it through here. Hey, that's funny. Look, it's coming out colors.

Rather than being put off by being contradicted, the teacher joins in the play and uses the opportune moment to show the boys more about the refraction of light. He moves from being a respondent to being an initiator. By showing the boys a spectrum he shifts them from one funny phenomenon to another one, one which, in this case, has more scientific significance.

TEACHER: That's right—now this way you should get a pretty good prism. [*Pause*] So that prism, or that spectrum, is just going to pass right through that water also.

LARRY: How come it doesn't turn back to white like it says?

TEACHER: Because it has to go back through the prism at the same angle it came out. If you get another prism, you can take that prism and so what you've got coming out is just the opposite of this—you get another beam of white light. Like I was saying the other day, that's how Newton proved that light is composed of colors.

LARRY: [*Gets another prism*] There—almost white.

TEACHER: Well, there's quite a difference between white and almost white, isn't there?

LARRY: I'll just move the prism a little.

The boys follow the teacher's move, we think, because he builds upon the knowledge they already have and because their curiosity has been aroused by the phenomenon presented.

We can also see the teacher developing the language that is used in scientific investigation. When confronted with a question, the teacher answers it by presenting his own train of thought. His wording—"if this comes . . . what you're doing is . . . and if that . . . and that is . . . it looks like . . . "—provides a model for the students to use in analyzing phenomena. The teacher then presents the boys with another phenomenon, giving them a situation in which they can use the model. He also subtly suggests the precise nature of scientific thinking when he challenges the boys with, "Well there's quite a difference between white and almost white, isn't there?" By introducing particular types and uses of language in a concrete context this teacher helps his students develop competence in the special language of science. In this case, the teacher started with what the students were talking about and then extended their discussion: This exchange illustrates how environments that support talk also support teaching.

Group Students for Instruction

Students need frequent opportunities to talk. The nature and size of groups in the classroom can significantly affect students' use of language. It's fair to say that the larger the group, the fewer opportunities individual students will have to use language. In general, whole-class discussions will never be a good way to encourage language use for many students, even though learning to talk in large groups is one of the skills students need to acquire in school. Large-group discussions tend to be dominated by more capable or outgoing students. And even if teachers can successfully involve most of the students in a whole-class discussion, it will be difficult to provide sufficient time to allow students to respond at length without seriously taxing the patience of the rest of the group. It is also hard for students to interact with each other in whole-class discussions, where talk tends to be channeled through the "teacher-as-loudspeaker" (Jones, 1988) and teachers devote a lot of time to calling students to attention or asking them to be quiet. Consequently, whole-class discussions offer students relatively few chances to interact with each other except through the teacher.

One of the best ways to encourage students to engage in extended discourse is to bring them together in small work and play groups. In our experience, groups of three to five tend to work best, but the optimum size depends on the task and the students in the group. Teachers will find that some students just don't work well together.

Ability grouping may appear to be an attractive way to encourage student participation in small groups, since students who lack confidence in their verbal ability may be shy about speaking in front of other, more fluent classmates. We know of one language-delayed student whose language was much more fluent when he worked with other children whose language ability was similar to his. But as a rule, the practice of grouping students by ability, particularly by language ability, does not promote language development. Mixed-ability groupings are more likely to extend the range of available audiences and language models. Less able students may sometimes be reluctant to speak up in the presence of those they perceive to be more able, but in our experience, students' reticence can be overcome if we design tasks that allow everyone to contribute. Open-ended tasks that do not stress right answers are especially likely to encourage student participation in small-group activities. As part of an "All About Me" unit, for example, one class of second graders made a collection of pictures and objects that were special to them to share with their classmates. When the time for sharing came, the children met in small rotating groups to talk about these collections. Under these conditions all the students had something to say.

In summary, the classroom environment can encourage students to use language by giving them things to talk about, opportunities to interact with each other, and assurances that what they say will be valued and accepted. But an effective physical setting isn't the only prerequisite for stimulating talk. Teachers must also manipulate the environment to expand the range of settings within which students use language, thus promoting their development as effective language users.

4 Using Language for a Variety of Purposes and Audiences

In the everyday world people don't just talk, they use language toward some end and in a context that almost always includes someone else. Of the two most important language goals in the classroom, one is to increase the range of functions for which students use language and the other is to vary and expand the audiences with whom students fulfill these purposes.

Using Language for Different Purposes

Teachers provide opportunities for students to use language for different purposes by creating situations that encourage all kinds of talk. Bringing a novel object into the classroom, such as a bird's nest or a quill pen, invites questioning and speculation. Construction activities may encourage planning (Staab, 1982; Tough, 1976). A reading lesson or a science experiment favors logical reasoning and predicting. A drama center or a puppet theater can inspire imaginary worlds and stories (Staab, 1982). Peer or cross-age tutoring situations put students in the teacher's shoes to discover what it's like to help someone else learn. Teachers who share their own experiences, favorite jokes, and stories invite their students to do the same.

It is important that teachers themselves have a strong sense of how language is used so that they can promote those uses in their classrooms. By observing and listening carefully to both children and adults as they talk and communicate during a typical day, teachers will get a good idea of the uses they are not hearing in their classrooms.

How teachers ask questions is an important factor in how students respond. Open-ended, probing questions, for example, invite students to speculate, imagine, and analyze.

27

In contrast, narrow questions with predictable answers only encourage students to use language to demonstrate their knowledge. And, of course, how teachers evaluate students' responses affects their willingness to use language for more sophisticated purposes, such as testing a hypothesis or logical reasoning, which carry a certain degree of risk.

But teachers don't need to contrive tasks to encourage students to use language. Often they only need to take advantage of opportunities that arise naturally during the school day. Students could help to plan an upcoming field-trip, for example, or work together as a group to solve a problem on the playground. We've already referred to the possibilities that present themselves when the class must determine its own rules for group work. In all these cases, involving students in talk makes good sense for teaching and planning as well as for learning.

The following excerpt (for which we are indebted to Glenda Barber) is a good example of a classroom discussion that becomes a forum for interacting through language. Three nine-year-old boys spend time in a withdrawal class to develop their language and literacy. As a part of this program they have produced a "big book," of which they are justifiably proud. They have now decided that they wish to put their book in the library to share with others. But this decision presents problems, which they attempt to solve with their teacher. The desire to share their work gives them a purpose, and their decisions affect how their work will be perceived and treated.

ADAM: That ... that ... that's what I was saying, but Mike said that ...

MARK: No. You guys said make a card so people could take it home.

BILL: I said that.

ADAM: Wait. First of all, first of all, first, we wanna keep it in the library and, that, and you said no.

MARK: Hey, we'll keep it. How 'bout the people who forget their books can look at that book over there.

ADAM: I wanna, I wanna ...

BILL: Can we leave it on the floor with other big books? 'Cause it's ... they ... no, no three, no, none of the people look at those big books.

MARK: So, you know where the little books are, like *Light in the Attic,* where the people ... we can put it there.

BILL: On the floor.

MIKE: The people forget their book, they can look at it.

BILL: They can put it on the floor.

ADAM: I don't want to do that. Actually, I want people to take it out.

BILL: Yeah, me too.

Two important aspects of this discussion are immediately apparent. The first is the commitment of the members of the group to the value of their book and their desire to share it. It is this commitment that makes the whole discussion possible. The boys are sure that people will enjoy their book and have no difficulty in considering it in the same terms as *Light in the Attic*. This pride leads to their next problem, which is how to share the book and still protect it. Their confidence and excitement are reflected in their speech patterns, such as Adam's repetition of "that . . . that . . . that's" and "first of all, first of all, first." These boys are wrestling with a real problem that requires them to devise creative solutions and work to build a consensus.

If teachers could maintain this level of authenticity in classrooms we are confident that much of the concern over language development would disappear from our schools. Linked to this commitment to authenticity is the role of the teacher. Nothing in this first excerpt indicates that the teacher is present, but she is. The students are talking to each other, they are not being prompted, and the teacher neither prods nor supervises their participation. She is remarkably patient. That is not to say that the teacher has no particular role, but she is in no hurry to take over ownership of either the problem or the solution. She is committed to assisting the boys in reaching a solution themselves.

TEACHER: Okay, but Michael has some concerns about that. Why don't you want people to take it home?

MARK: 'Cause, I don't like people wrecking it in case they ripped a page, or if they have baby brothers then they can rip it or tear it or cut it.

BILL: But you still have to share with other people except for us.

TEACHER: Uh huh.

MARK: Okay, let's see. You take it out, and I bet if they have a little brother, they'll cut it or something.

BILL: Just say "no baby brothers," or something.

MARK: Oh yeah.

TEACHER: Is there something that we could put on here to make sure?

BILL: "Keep it away from baby brothers."

MARK: Yeah, but say their mother isn't home and their dad's working.

TEACHER: Look at the size of this book. Is there a problem with taking it home?

BILL: You can.

ADAM: As long as . . . Make . . . Put on a sign: "If you do not have a bag, do not take this book out," or something like that, "because you could get it ripped or torn."

MARK: That's a good idea.

BILL: And you can put, "No, don't take it out if it's raining if you don't have a bag."

ADAM: That's what I said. Don't even take it out either because like, it could get scratched.

This part of the discussion clearly defines the issue. Mark is concerned that when people take the book out of the library, it might be damaged. The other boys remind him that the work must be shared and that they want it shared. The teacher has helped the group identify the problem. It also appears that the teacher is trying to hint at solutions to the problem when she asks "Is there something we could put on here?" and (referring to the book's size) "Is there a problem with taking it home?" The boys don't really pick up on either question, misunderstanding the first and ignoring the second, but the teacher lets them go their own way. The boys are able to create a variety of possible scenarios that allow them to express the problems they see.

TEACHER: That's sort of like all books though, isn't it? Like what you're saying for this book should apply for all the books in the library, shouldn't it?

ADAM: Yeah.

BILL: Keep away from the baby.

TEACHER: Well, if there is a problem with taking it home . . . because when you take it home, let somebody take it home, you really don't control how they treat it, do you?

ADAM: Why don't we try it for one week and see what happens?

TEACHER: The other solution was what Mark said, to keep it here and put a sign on it that just says, "For Library Use Only," in other words, when people come.

MARK: If it rips . . .

TEACHER: When people come to the library, they can look at it, but they don't necessarily have to take it home.

ADAM: That's a good idea. Why don't you put . . .

MARK: But if it rips . . .

ADAM: "For Teachers Only," or something like that, for them to read, you know, like to a class.

TEACHER: Like the other big books.

ADAM: Like that *Napping House.*

TEACHER: The way the other big books are.

MARK: But if we'll try it out, then if, if some, if it rips or something, we may have to fix it, because I never wanted them to take it home and they did.

Using Mark's ideas the teacher seems to move the boys into backing down from their desire to let the book be taken out. The boys recall other books that have the "For Teachers Only" label on them. It's not surprising that they should take this protective approach to their own book—after all, they made it. But then the commitment to sharing that was so marked at the beginning of the discussion reemerges, and the boys move from talking about how to protect the book to how to make it available. It is this commitment, and their sense that this is a *real* discussion, where they are truly making a decision, that allows the boys to disregard the teacher's suggestion and search for their own solution.

ADAM: There's one problem with taking that book home . . . is . . . like, like, with Robert Munsch, they have hundreds of copies of their books, you know, like it isn't like you can . . . Can you photocopy that? Oh yeah, you have to have color photocopy.

TEACHER: I can't photocopy it that size. You know, it's awful big.

MARK: Make it a little book and then people can take it out.

ADAM: What you need is a color photocopy.

MARK: Oh, I have an idea. You can . . .

BILL: Oh, I know . . .

MARK: You can photocopy it little and put it in the library and people can take it out.

ADAM: Yeah.

BILL: I think, no.

TEACHER: That would be a good idea, Mark, but I can't make it any smaller than that.

BILL: But I think, I think I can, we can go like this. Make a big copy and a little copy of it so little people can bring it home and big people who want to take it home, they can take it home, the big book.

TEACHER: Yes, I think Bill has a point too, because if you want to take the time to make a little copy of that, we can circulate that in the library.

ADAM: That's actually worse because little kids normally lose it, but big kids won't, but that book's . . . it should be the opposite actually.

MARK: But, you know what we should do, we should make a little book and then put it in the library so people could take it home.

TEACHER: That's what Bill said.

MARK: Then, let's make a little one of it, the same thing.

TEACHER: If you want to.

Adam moves the group toward a final solution by identifying the key problem with class-made books: they are unique and, unlike commercial books, irreplaceable. This leads the group to consider producing a second copy, which could be borrowed from the library while the original is preserved.

The group jumps on this solution and with the teacher's help works out the details.

BILL: But I think we should make it a little bit longer.

ADAM: Can't you go downtown and get it color photocopied? Isn't there anyone . . .

TEACHER: I don't think so.

MARK: It's too late to go downtown and get it photocopied.

ADAM: Isn't there one downtown?

TEACHER: If you make a little copy of it, I could make copies of the little copy, but I can't . . .

ADAM: In color?

TEACHER: But I can't make copies of big . . .

ADAM: In color?

TEACHER: No, you'd have to color it yourself.

ADAM: We could do that.

BILL: Yeah.

MARK: Fine.

TEACHER: But you'd have to make a little book.

ADAM: The problem is, doesn't it just come out the outlines? Because last time, when my mom photocopied a book from the library, there's a cooking recipe, right, and it came out like, when you color this in, this came out all blurry.

TEACHER: Yes.

ADAM: If you wanted to do that, you couldn't, this would come all black, actually.

TEACHER: Well, what you would do is draw the outlines of everything in your little book, and I would photocopy it like that, and then you'd do, you'd have to color each one.

This is a successful discussion in that it leads to the resolution of a problem. It is also successful because the boys have all been actively engaged in using language. Throughout the discussion, the boys are very focused. Each response fits with what has gone before. If the boys don't always acknowledge each other's contributions, they recognize similar ideas when they have been repeated. Since they are under some pressure to make their concerns and solutions clearly understood, they revise what they have already said and use examples to illustrate their points. As a result, there is a fine precision and shading in their speech. Adam, for example, presents his concern by saying, "*actually,* I want people to take it out." Mark counters this later by saying, "Yeah, *but say* their mother isn't home. . . . " We can see Bill struggle for this precision as he outlines the solution, "*But I think,* I think I can, *we can go like this.* Make a big copy and a little copy of it *so little people can* bring it home *and big people* who want to take it home, they can take it home, *the big book.*" Clearly the boys are using the widest possible range of syntactic resources here, stretching themselves as language users in the process.

The discussion encourages the boys to use the language of logic and speculation. They build arguments and create alternative possibilities. Yet it is this use of language as a tool of abstract thought that is often cited as a major problem for those students having difficulty in school. In this specific, personal setting, however, the boys use this type of language easily and effectively because the situation supports its use. We see again how good language situations nudge students to extend their language and at the same time supply a context that supports this extended language use.

By separating talk from purpose we render students incapable of self-evaluation. In discussions like these, students do not need an external evaluation of their language. They know what they intend to achieve and can judge whether or not they are achieving it. Their attempts to clarify their meaning demonstrate the extent to which they monitor what they say. As long as talk is an outgrowth of intention, students can judge the effectiveness of their own language.

Using Language for Different Audiences

Last summer six-year-old Anne and her family visited the Province of Prince Edward Island. Shortly after they arrived on Prince Edward Island Anne met an adult who asked her where she was from. She responded, "I'm from Canada." To which the adult replied, "Welcome to the Kingdom of Prince Edward Island!"

Everyone got a good laugh out of this incident. Part of the humor resulted from the fact that Anne didn't realize she was still in Canada. The other problem was that from the listener's perspective Anne's response wasn't very helpful and seemed, therefore, a bit of a joke. The adult expected a more specific reply, like "Toronto" or perhaps even "Ontario." It's like asking someone who they are and having them answer "a girl"— humorous, perhaps, but not informative. A slightly older child wouldn't have made the mistake Anne did. They would have recognized intuitively that, since they were in Canada and the person asking the question was Canadian, something more specific than "I'm from Canada" was required. Or if they had made such a mistake, they would have realized from the listener's response that something was wrong and attempted to figure out and "repair" the breakdown in communication.

Whenever we open our mouths to speak we make assumptions about the background knowledge of our listeners. Do they speak English? Are they interested in football? Will they understand the sentence structure and vocabulary we're using? We do this unconsciously and easily, as evidenced by our ability to adjust our language automatically when we are speaking to small children. Our assessment of the listener's needs will affect both the form (for example, vocabulary and syntactic complexity) and the content of our language. And we're constantly reassessing the needs of the listener as the conversation proceeds, perhaps providing additional expla- nation if we sense confusion or changing topics altogether if we conclude that a particular topic isn't of interest. Speakers also adjust the form of their language (that is, syntax, choice of vocabulary) in accordance with their assessment of a lis- tener's needs and status. Requests directed at those judged to have higher status are likely to be more polite ("May I have another muffin?") than the same request directed at someone of equal or lower status ("Hand me another muffin, would you?"). A listener's status will also affect the relative formality of a speaker's speech. It's likely that students will use more formal forms with their teachers ("No, Miss Evans, I didn't like it") than with their friends ("Hey, man, that really sucks"). Any competent language user is able to adjust the form and content of what they say in accordance with what they perceive the needs of their listener to be, and these can vary according to the listener's background knowledge and relationship to the speaker (that is, relative status and famil- iarity).

Both children and adults occasionally misjudge the needs of their audience although adults are usually better at chang- ing course and avoiding misunderstandings. It is often much more transparent when children misjudge the needs of their listeners and, as in the example of Anne above, this is usu- ally a source of amusement to adults. Still, even young chil- dren have a strong sense that a speaker's language choices are affected by who the intended listener is. When Anne was five, she and her one-year-old brother, Ian, were riding in the backseat of the car. As they were riding along their mother pointed out the window and said, "Look at the cows." Not even looking up from the picture she was coloring, Anne casually replied, "Ian's asleep." From Anne's perspective, the content of this talk coming from her mother was unlikely to be appropriate to her, a five-year-old, so Mom must have been talking to her younger brother.

Children (and adults) learn to consider the needs of differ- ent audiences when they talk by participating in conversa- tions with a variety of people of differing background, status, and familiarity relative to them as speakers. In the unlikely event that a child comes to school having only experienced her parents as listeners, that child will only know how to adapt her language to the differing needs of her mother and father. Similarly, if children in school only talk with their teachers, all they will learn is how to communicate with teachers. Although students will, of course, be exposed to a variety of audiences outside school, regardless of what their teachers do, some children, especially those whose language learning is lagging behind their peers, will benefit from being exposed to a range of potential communicative partners.

Teachers who engage their students in genuine conversation (see Chapter 8) provide one audience for student talk. But the most obvious and convenient audiences are other students. Students who work in pairs and small groups experience a variety of audiences within the context of normal classroom routines. Students in other classrooms are another potential source of audiences. In a number of schools, seventh- and eighth-grade students work regularly with first- and second-grade students, often collaborating with them on writing or art projects. In this context the older students must develop language appropriate to directing and assisting younger children whose background knowledge and language is different from theirs. The first-grade children must speak explicitly enough to communicate their experience and intentions to older children. It would also be a valuable experience for first- and second-grade students to work with younger students (that is, kindergarteners or first-graders). Successful students are often asked to tutor less able students, and this makes immediate sense, since we assume that good students have the necessary understanding that we wish them to share. We should realize however, that often the one who benefits most from tutoring is the student who is providing the leadership. One advantage of having older children work with younger children is that students having problems have a chance to operate in the role of teacher. In one situation we know of, older students who themselves had been referred for remedial help were used as reading partners for younger children who were having difficulty reading. The teacher found that the confidence and insight into reading these students gained as tutors became a major factor in their own development as readers.

It's more difficult for children in school to experience a variety of adult audiences, but it's not impossible. If students interview people in their community they can gather valuable information for their assignments while at the same time gaining the opportunity to talk with different audiences. A classroom unit on occupations, for example, can be supplemented with student interviews with people in the local community about their jobs. Another way to expand students' experience with mature audiences is to invite adults into the classroom. Increasing the participation of parents in the classroom is one way to do this, but if parents are going to expand children's language experiences they must have the opportunity to interact with students individually as well as in small groups. Recently retired people are another resource, and they can also provide valuable assistance to classroom teachers in other ways, such as reading to and with students or responding to students' writing. Jones (1988) argues that for some students it would be valuable to have a regularly scheduled school session during which they join an adult in the community in a support and learning capacity.

Writing can be another important source of information about the role of audience, assuming that students have regular opportunities to write for audiences other than their teachers. Writers must pay particularly close attention to the needs of their audiences, since audience feedback is often delayed and writers usually do not have a chance to clarify what they have said. Potential audiences for student writing (such as letters or "published" stories) include students in the same class, students in other classes, pen pals, and people in the community, for example, residents of nursing homes.

In the classroom, the teacher has a key role as a language-environment builder. That environment is shaped by the purposes for which students use language and the kinds of audiences available to them. When we successfully introduce authentic purposes and varied audiences into classroom talk we, in effect, introduce our students to powerful new language teachers.

5 Encouraging Extended Conversations

We've been encouraging teachers to create classrooms that provide children with opportunities to talk with them and with one another. Indeed, although we hope children will experience a variety of audiences, the reality of the classroom is that much of the talk that takes place will be between the teacher and the student. In this chapter we wish to consider the teacher's role in ensuring that this interaction is beneficial.

In their work on classroom language, Connie and Harold Rosen (1973) discuss the important role of the teacher in developing language through sustained conversation.

> Where does the teacher come in? Is she ever, as some have suggested, reduced to a silent onlooker and head-patter content to assume all must be well if only the children are chattering away? My experience suggests that there are kinds of talk that are fanned into life and sustained by the teacher. There is a nice paradox here. The teacher in this role urges into articulation what was only half-formed and moves children towards new verbal ambitions. Such attempts might never occur in their own group talk or at best be fleeting. Yet by virtue of the fact that a teacher has made such things possible she has also added important items to the children's repertoire so they can in fact use them when the teacher is no longer present. From the long-term point of view her role is to render herself obsolete. As children internalize her verbal strategies they need her intervention less and less. (43)

To help students develop these strategies, teachers need to encourage them to engage in extended conversational interactions. Here students may initiate talk themselves, take extended conversational turns, or take multiple turns. In this way, they try out their language skills and extend their knowledge of how to use language in conversational settings.

The reality in many classrooms, however, is that many students are reluctant to talk in class and, when they do speak, they often limit themselves to short answers. It's easy to point to factors such as personality (that is, shyness) or language ability to explain this reticence, but there are also a number of other factors that can affect children's willingness to try out their language in class. Two key factors that can potentially affect the quantity and quality of students' language are the nature of teachers' invitations to students to talk and the nature of teachers' responses to students' talk.

Inviting Students to Talk

Sometimes classroom discussions are virtually over before they begin. They end with a teacher's decision to ask questions that, by their very nature, limit students' response. These questions invite students to supply an answer that usually requires just a few words (for example, Teacher: "Why did the Pilgrims come to America?" Student: "They wanted to be free"). Other questions, to which the teacher obviously already knows the answer, are clearly evaluative (for example, "What happened in the story I just read you?"). These questions discourage lengthy student responses, since the more they say the more likely it is they'll say something wrong.

Much attention has been given in the research literature to the limitations of questions that can be answered in a word or two. Consequently, teachers have learned to ask more general, open-ended questions in an effort to encourage lengthier student responses. Question taxonomies have also been developed to help teachers proceed from lower- to higher-level questions. Undoubtedly this emphasis has helped teachers ask better questions. But what concerns us is that asking better questions can become an end in itself instead of a means to an end. After all, the proof of the pudding isn't the form of the question but the quality of the response.

Planning lively and productive discussions with students does not begin with formulating the right questions. It begins with the teacher's reasons for the discussion, from which questions or other teacher invitations to talk should flow naturally. If the teacher's purpose is to evaluate whether students have learned certain facts related to the curriculum, then questions that can be answered with a short response or a yes or no may be most appropriate. But if teachers are interested in engaging students in extended dialogue to expand their language potential, then they must convey a genuine interest in finding out what students have to say. We once observed a seventh-grade teacher who began a whole-class discussion of the books the students had been reading by asking a boy, "Another gory book, eh John? What do you see in those books?" The student then gave a fairly lengthy response. The key here wasn't the form of the question. The student could easily have said something like, "I just like 'em." But through the tone of her voice and her body language, the teacher conveyed a genuine interest in what John had to say—she really wanted to know, so he told her.

This teacher had won her students' trust that she was sincerely interested in what they had to say over the course of the school year. The question "What do you see in those books?" might not have elicited much talk earlier in the year, when students might have been unsure of her motivation in asking such a question (Is this a test? Does she want to know if I got the right—that is, her—meaning? Is she going to tell me I shouldn't read this kind of book?). And we think it's fair to say that the older the students, the more difficult it will be for us as teachers to convince them that we really care to hear what they have to say. Experienced students are more likely to recall times when this wasn't the case. So, one reason students may not share their honest opinions with us is that their previous experience has not convinced them that we're always genuinely interested in what they have to say.

Responding to Students' Language

Teachers can get talk started, but an equally important factor in promoting extended discourse in the classroom is how they respond to children's talk. A teacher's response can influence students' language development. By encouraging students to say more, both in the present and the future, teachers can expand students' opportunities to use language and learn how language is used. The teacher who hears a student's story about the death of his dog and says, "Your dog's death made you very sad," not only indicates that he heard what the student was saying but also invites the student to say more. The teacher's interest may also encourage that student to feel more confident about initiating talk in the future. But the emphasis should not be on the mechanics of responding (for example, mechanically echoing what the speaker has said, as in "active listening") but on demonstrating a genuine interest in children's words and ideas. Again, the emphasis should be on communication. In general, nothing ensures talk so much as the presence of an interested listener.

Conversely, entering into a dialogue with children for reasons other than communication will usually have a chilling effect on their language. Evaluative responses (for example, "Jason, the word is ran, not runned"), especially in response to child-initiated language, tend to discourage children from talking. When we evaluate someone's language we indirectly tell him that we are more interested in his correct use of form than in what he wants to tell us. Readers who doubt the negative effect of this kind of evaluation might reflect on the reaction of their spouse or a close friend if they were to correct that person's grammar or comment on the quality of expression.

Sometimes teachers enter into conversations with students in order to highlight what they believe is important in children's experience or to develop certain conversational styles, such as narrative. The following excerpt from a first-grade Show-and-Tell session taken from Searle (1984, 481–82) is illustrative:

TEACHER: Oh, boy! What's that?

TEACHER: Maybe you'll explain to us about what this is. [*To class*] If you know, don't tell. Would you turn right around so we can all hear?

DAVE: A walkie-talkie.

TEACHER: Do you just have one of them? How many do you have?

DAVE: One.

TEACHER: How many do you need to listen?

DAVE: Two. My brother has one.

TEACHER: I see. Can you show us how it works? You turn it on first. Is this where you turn it on?

DAVE: Um, that's where I talk to my brother.

TEACHER: I see. That's called the [*unintelligible*]. That's where you can talk to you brother. I don't imagine you can talk to him now. Did he bring his to school?

DAVE: [*Shakes his head*]

TEACHER: And how do you talk? Let's pretend that Chris is talking. No? You are not going to show us? How many have used a walkie-talkie?

Show-and-Tell is presumably a time when children can talk about what interests them. But in this example, the teacher does most of the talking, taking control of the content and the direction of the conversation. Here Show-and-Tell becomes "student shows and teacher tells" (Dillon and Searle, 1981). Questions like "Do you have just one of them?" or "Can you show us how this works?" divert the student from his own interests and focus instead on the teacher's understanding. Alternative questions like "What can you tell us about it?" would have encouraged the student to share his perspective. Then, through the response of an interested audience, more talk might have followed. Similarly, follow-up comments like "That sounds like fun. I'd like to try. Show me how it works" would have kept the child in charge of his language, an important factor in language development. By taking control of a student's language teachers risk limiting student contributions to the interaction and invalidating students' background experience and perspective. Rather than learning to use language to fulfill their own intentions, students learn what teachers regard as important for them to say and think.

Responding effectively to children's language requires that teachers be aware of the experiences on which children are basing their talk. Consider the following example:

A teacher of young children was once alarmed by a violent and apparently chaotic game her boys were playing. As she disciplined them she realized that the game was based on a new TV cartoon show. That night she watched the show and the next day, rather than disciplining the students, she was able to talk about the characters with them, and more importantly, she was able to enter into the game, directing it from within. (Dudley-Marling and Searle, 1988, 142)

Teachers who respond to children's conversational intentions also model effective conversational behavior for their students. They demonstrate how to use language to make meaning, how to take the reactions of others into account, how to hold the floor, and how to share as a listener.

We see an example of this kind of modeling in one teacher's "news time." Mrs. Painter sits on a chair in front of the group and invites student participation. Students raise their hands and, when recognized by her, present their news. In the typical session that follows, David, who has been sick, has brought in a metal kidney-shaped dish as a souvenir of his hospital stay.

TEACHER: We're glad David's back at school.

DAVID: Yeah.

TEACHER: You were quite sick David.

DAVID: Um hmm.

CHILDREN: What was wrong with him?

TEACHER: Well I think he's going to show us something that he's brought with him now that he has his shoes on.

DAVID: Should I get up there? and um . . . ?

TEACHER: Yeah. Why don't you, hmm?

CLARA: Ah, you know my dad took it to work to get the money.

TEACHER: All right.

DAVID: I don't know what the thing is called. It's a . . . or something.

TEACHER: What's it for?

DAVID: Mm . . . [*Long pause*]

TEACHER: Where did you get it David?

DAVID: Hm? From the hospital.

TEACHER: What do you think this is for?

DAVID: Some kind of dish.

TEACHER: Um hmm. Partly that or if you're just lying down and you really feel sick and you need to spit up a little bit. You had a bad cold or if you were sick at your stomach. It's for people who have to be in their bed and can't get up quickly. And they let you bring this home did they?

DAVID: Um hmm.

TEACHER: Um hmm. What hospital were you in David?

DAVID: Um, a general hospital I think.

TEACHER: You think so? Was it Sick Kids? [*Local nickname for Sick Children's Hospital*]

DAVID: Yeah, I think.

TEACHER: All right. Well, where are you going to put that?

MILES: Did he have to go to sleep?

TEACHER: Do you mean like an anesthetic?

MILES: Yeah.

TEACHER: I don't think so. I think they just checked him out.

MILES: I hate that, because I got a lot of my blood . . .

TEACHER: Hmm?

MILES: . . . scrape it.

TEACHER: Yes, sometimes they do take your blood before you have an anesthetic just to . . .

MELISSA: You know . . . only do that.

TEACHER: Not to take a sample of your blood?

MELISSA: Yeah.

TEACHER: Yeah, I think you're right. Your dad could tell you about that. Mmm?

EDWARD: One time I . . . the hospital missed my vein. They couldn't find the vein to put it in.

TEACHER: Isn't that provoking when that happens?

EDWARD: Yeah.

TEACHER: And they try and try?

EDWARD: Mm hmm?

TEACHER: And I think the harder you try to help them the harder it gets for them to find the vein 'cause you get tense.

EDWARD: Yeah.

TEACHER: That's happened to me before and do you know what they had to do once was use a child's needle. It's a smaller needle. They couldn't get a sample of my blood no matter what they did so they said, "We'll get a pediatric needle" and, that's a child's 'cause it was smaller, so I know what that's like. Yes Sally?

SALLY: I went to get my tonsils out.

TEACHER: Yes?

SALLY: . . . like, um . . . I had about, let's see, three needles. One when I first came in . . .

TEACHER: Um hmm.

SALLY: One when I was in the waiting room for a nurse to come to take . . . and then the other night I got a needle. I went out to get my operation.

TEACHER: I see.

DAVID: I had two needles.

TEACHER: Yes . . .

DAVID: . . . one sleeping one and two . . .

TEACHER: Right.

DAVID: . . . they, they said instead of me having a sleeping needle they'd . . . and that's what they did. They just gave me . . .

TEACHER: I see.

CLARA: Isn't that mean 'cause when I woke up I remember it was on so when I was moving my arms to stretch and it's so . . . and it made my arm a little bit heavier.

TEACHER: Yes?

CLARA: It hurts because I'm pulling the tubes . . .

TEACHER: Right.

CLARA: . . . and the needle.

TEACHER: Well I think all of us are happy when that's finished and we don't have to have an anesthetic.

The discussion growing out of David's report is quite extensive and involves many of the students in the group. They get more news of David's experience, share their own personal experience of sickness and hospitals, and call upon their own knowledge of hospital procedure. The teacher herself extends David's explanation, coordinates responses, listens carefully to the students, and shares her personal reactions and experiences. She plays a major role in the activity. Although her authority and right to control the discussion are acknowledged and exercised, her method and approach are oriented primarily to the content of the talk. Her response to the child who reported the experience of the missed vein illustrates her orientation to content. Her first response, "Isn't that provoking when that happens," is emotional. Her second response, "And they try and try," appears to be an invitation for the child to continue, or at least to keep the topic alive. Her final response is an extensive personal anecdote. There is a high rate of participation: even in this short excerpt, Mrs. Painter speaks with five of the eight children in the group. Throughout the discussion, she engages her students in extended conversational interactions while demonstrating effective conversational behavior.

Part of the art of conversation is knowing when not to respond or, at least, when to delay response. The literature on classroom language indicates that teachers often wait only a second for students to formulate a response to teacher initiations (Honea, 1982; Lehr, 1984) and perhaps even less time than that for lower-achieving students (Good, 1980). Increasing wait-time to as little as three to five seconds can increase the length of student responses, the amount of student-initiated talk, the frequency of student interactions, and the use of speculative thinking (Honea, 1982; Rowe, in Hassler, 1979). Many students, especially those who may be struggling to learn language, have difficulty formulating a response in less than a second. By increasing the amount of time we give students to respond, we enable them to formulate more thoughtful responses and often find that they know much more than we thought.

We wish to encourage extended interactions between teacher and student, not because extended talk is in itself an end but because, by supporting and encouraging students to produce extended conversation, we are allowing them to develop linguistic strategies that will make it possible for them to use language with increasing effectiveness. Teachers are more successful in this endeavor when their focus is personal and interested and when they are responsive to the intentions of their students. To maintain such a focus is not a matter of applying mechanistic formulas. It is, rather, the art of authentic conversation.

6 Strategic Approaches for Teaching Language

The major goal of classroom language instruction, as we've said, is to increase the range of purposes for which students use language and the settings in which they can fulfill these intentions. The primary means of achieving this goal is to immerse students in language, to give them experience in using language with a variety of audiences and in a variety of physical settings. This immersion in language demonstrates to students what language is for and how it is used while, at the same time, inviting them to try out language themselves. As they struggle to use language in different communicative settings, they learn, without explicit instruction, most of the words, the word-ordering rules, and the conversational rules (such as getting and maintaining the floor, turn taking, and so on) they need to represent their understanding of the world and get things done with language. They also learn the effect that audience and setting have on language use.

We do not wish to suggest that all students will use language with equal degrees of success in all these tasks. As teachers observe students, they may discover that some children appear to have difficulty with relatively specific aspects of language and that this difficulty interferes with their ability to use language effectively in one or more settings. In fact, in classrooms that feature lots of talk, specific difficulties are more apt to make themselves apparent. If children have trouble with syntactic rules or vocabulary, for example, they may find it difficult to understand and be understood in the classroom; if they are unable to get the conversational floor, they may have fewer opportunities to participate in conversations. In the same way, if children have difficulty with topic maintenance and turn taking, they may risk social rejection by their peers; if they have problems understanding how language works in the classroom, they may find it hard to follow classroom routines. Some students, for example, do not know what their teachers want when they say, "All eyes up here."

In cases such as these, teachers—especially those whose classrooms include students who are struggling to use language effectively—may make a more deliberate effort to address the particular areas that seem to interfere with students' use of language. In addition to creating rich language-learning environments in their classrooms, teachers may wish to focus on specific language goals, such as students' understanding of idioms, multiple-meaning words, or passive sentences.

In this chapter we discuss a strategic approach to language teaching. This approach enables teachers to address the specific language needs of their students within a context of sound language-learning principles.

The Nature of Strategic Teaching

Strategic teaching begins with the identification of real and important needs. When specific goals emerge from the ongoing interaction of the classroom, they are more apt to be goals that are shared by students. Because students see how a specific aspect of language can contribute to their own legitimate needs, they are already motivated to pay attention, and the teacher is assured that there will be opportunities for students to develop this specific aspect of language through use.

But specific goals do not, in our view, indicate specific (that is, clinical) teaching. Even if students are having difficulty learning a particular aspect of language, the nature of what they are learning does not change. Language learning can never be reduced to a collection of discrete skills because language isn't a collection of skills. What language users learn is a code that allows them to represent their worldview and communicate it. The form and content of language always occur simultaneously with its use and must be learned simultaneously; they cannot be fragmented for purposes of instruction. Moreover, language is always used in some context and must be learned in context. In other words, the general guidelines for language learning outlined earlier still apply.

How do teachers go about addressing specific features of language? As we've said, it's our view that the best approach to teaching specific aspects of language is strategic, not clinical. Teachers encourage language learning by placing students in contexts that are especially likely to highlight and encourage particular aspects of language. A baking activity can highlight the use of both present and past tense forms, since the participants will naturally refer to both ongoing (Mary is stirring) and completed actions (Justin poured . . .). Similarly, construction materials like Lego or Tinkertoys might encourage the use of action words, such as *make, build, join,* and spatial prepositions, such as *on, under, next to.* So the idea isn't to teach isolated aspects of language directly, it is to make a more deliberate effort to challenge children to use certain kinds of language by increasing their exposure to particular language demonstrations in situations that call up and support the meaning.

Which aspects of language do we address? If we decide to encourage proficiency in specific aspects of language we should focus on those language features that interfere with students' ability to get their needs met in particular settings. In other words, we should encourage the use of specific forms or words only as a means of supporting what students themselves are trying to do with language. If we determine students' needs by using a scope and sequence schema and a formal or informal test of language skills, we may end up teaching students skills just because we feel they don't know them, not because they need them. If students don't have personal reasons for learning language our efforts are unlikely to succeed, as is evident in the often futile efforts of parents and teachers to teach children irregular past tense forms (for example, *ran* instead of *runned*).

Examples of Strategic Teaching

In the rest of this chapter we'll illustrate strategic approaches to teaching language in the classroom by discussing how teachers might go about encouraging students to learn about words, word-ordering rules, and narrative skills. We chose these topics not because we feel that these are the only skills that must be addressed but because they can provide examples of strategic approaches generally.

LEARNING WORDS

Like adults, children learn the words they need to fulfill their communicative intentions and get along in their communities. The actual words children learn—their vocabulary—is a function of their environment and their previous experiences. All children come to school with a considerable range of experiences, although not the same ones, which accounts for most of the differences in their expressive and receptive vocabularies. Children whose families do a lot of traveling, for example, learn words associated with travel (*exit, motel, billboard*). Children who enjoy baking with their fathers and mothers learn words identified with baking, such as *rise, yeast, mix*. Children who participate in sports learn sports words (*offense, defense*). If children watch their parents practice a specialized craft like silversmithing, they will learn terms associated with silversmithing, such as *pitch, planish*, and *pickle*. Similarly, children from culturally different backgrounds will have experiences and vocabulary different from their teachers and classmates.

In general, the more varied people's experiences, the richer and more varied their vocabularies, although some experiences and therefore some vocabularies, are more likely to match the expectations of teachers and schools. Students' vocabularies, like their experiences, aren't necessarily impoverished, only different. But these differences can interfere with their ability to get along in school.

Teachers who deliberately provide interesting activities for their students in the classroom or on field trips also encourage vocabulary development *if students are also given the opportunity to talk about their experiences.* Children do not learn words by memorizing formal definitions based on somebody else's judgments about their needs and somebody else's experience. They learn words by trying them out, by using them to represent their experiences and make sense of their world. L. S. Vygotsky (1986) indicated that the ability to use a word based on a partial understanding helps us extend *our* meaning. Similarly, Marland (1977) states, "Only *use* can help a pupil take possession of words and the use must be in a variety of real situations" (185). We can't give children words but we can encourage them to use words by inviting them to participate in interesting and meaningful activities.

Almost all teachers are interested in general vocabulary enrichment, but they may also want to help students gain control over particular words (such as subject vocabulary) or classes of words (such as abstract nouns). Teachers can promote more specific vocabulary development—encouraging students to learn to use particular words or classes of words, including idioms and words with multiple meanings—by involving students in specific experiences or taking advantage of opportunities for vocabulary development that arise naturally during the day. For example, an informal discussion about fighting on the playground may help students learn the meaning of expressions like "chill out" or "backing down." Inviting students to write letters or talk on the telephone—where speakers and listeners cannot see each other —encourages students to use more specific referents. In general, teachers facilitate vocabulary development by encouraging students to participate in activities that highlight certain words or kinds of words and challenging students to test the meanings of words for themselves.

In addition to developing an adequate general vocabulary, getting along in school also requires that students learn the specialized vocabulary associated with math, science, social studies, and other school subjects. Teachers expect students to be able to use and understand terms like *compare* and *contrast, add* and *subtract, import* and *export, afferent* and *efferent,* and so on, which allow for a precise discussion of subject matter. But if teachers give in to the temptation to give these words to their students, students will be burdened with learning both the words and the concepts they represent at the same time. A more effective approach, we believe, is to share more formal subject vocabulary with students only after they have first come to an understanding of the concepts represented by subject vocabulary in their own language. Teachers, for example, may postpone introducing terms like *add, subtract, divide,* or *regroup* until students have come to grips with these concepts in the context of their own background experience.

PUTTING WORDS TOGETHER

Syntax is a tool for coding or representing experience. Children's syntax becomes increasingly complex as they use language to meet their needs in a range of settings and to represent their increasingly complex view of the world. Syntactic structures are tools, means to an end. The actual structures we use and learn are related to certain kinds of thinking, certain purposes, and certain language contexts. From this perspective it isn't surprising that spurts of language growth in young children are often associated with interesting experiences, a visit to a museum or a trip to the zoo, for example. Children's language is stretched as they try to represent what for them are important and interesting events. Personal involvement is also a factor in the complexity of children's language. Cazden (1970) concludes that "the greater the degree of affect or personal involvement in the topic of conversation, the greater the likelihood of structural complexity" (259).

Teachers can facilitate students' syntactic development by exposing them to a wide range of syntactic structures and by challenging them to tap their latent linguistic resources (Rosen and Rosen, 1973) to represent their experiences. But teachers do not need to depend on relatively unusual events like trips to the museum or the zoo, although these may be useful. Nor does the teacher's focus on oral language development need to be (or should it be) separate from the rest of the curriculum. Reading, writing, math, science, and social studies all have the potential to excite children's interest and stretch their linguistic abilities. But the potential of school learning to do this depends on how well it fulfills students' needs and satisfies their natural curiosity. Reading, for example, can be a means of gathering information as well as a source of pleasure. Writing can be used to record information, to communicate, and to create art. Science and social studies are tools that enable students to make sense of the natural and social worlds. In this way, school learning expands students' experience, fulfills their personal needs, and, through discussion and sharing, challenges them to stretch their language. In contrast, because it gives students little incentive to talk and little to talk about, a curriculum that emphasizes the learning of isolated skills and subskills does not challenge students' language potential. Ironically, the emphasis on routine and the rigidly controlled environment common in many classes for special education students will be especially unlikely to stimulate language learning.

Teachers may call forth more specific types of language structures by providing students with particular kinds of experiences. For example, the manipulation of materials while investigating some phenomenon, such as what makes bubbles appear when you blow through a straw into a liquid, may stimulate the use of *if-then* and *so-because* constructions. An informal discussion of personal experiences may encourage the use of idioms ("Mark *made fun of* me") or metaphors ("She *broke down* and cried"). A simulated news broadcast is likely to call forth formal, standard English.

In general, when students have the opportunity to discuss experience that is rich and varied, they use increasingly complex language. Occasionally, teachers or language specialists may employ more deliberate strategies to highlight or model syntax for students. We have learned from the literature on early parent-child language interactions, for example, that parents often expand children's language into adult forms and model language forms (Child: "Mommy, bird pretty." Mother: "Yes, the bird is pretty [expansion] and he's eating the seeds from the bird feeder, isn't he?" [modeling]). Undoubtedly, these are useful language lessons, but as we noted when describing language learning, only in retrospect. When parents are talking with their children, their focus is on communication, not on explicitly teaching language. When we try to emulate the language "teaching" strategies of parents with our students, we enter into conversation with them for ulterior reasons. Our emphasis on teaching is probably transparently obvious to most school-age children. What may be an expansion or a model to an adult may from the child's perspective be an evaluation, which will likely discourage language use, not promote it. The skillful and judicious use of techniques like modeling and expansion may occasionally be effective but should, in our opinion, be used with caution.

TELLING STORIES

Most teachers, especially primary teachers, are interested in getting students to construct a good narrative, to relate stories or events in their lives, in a clear and orderly manner. This is usually one of the primary goals of Show-and-Tell or sharing times. But some students don't seem to catch on, and this lack of understanding may interfere with their written stories as well as their narrative accounts during formal sharing times.

For students to learn how to exploit the narrative function of language, at least two things have to happen. They have to be exposed to regular demonstrations of how narrative works; in other words, they have to have the "data." And they have to have frequent opportunities to try out the narrative function themselves by telling stories. Of course, this "trying out" is how children (and adults) learn about any aspect of language.

When children talk outside of the classroom, their conversations are filled with stories. Children's narratives may be fairly rare during school hours, however (Clarke, 1990), perhaps because constraints on time and the formality of lessons limit their opportunities to share stories. Sharing times or Show-and-Tell sessions are the most obvious attempts by teachers to encourage "orderly" story-telling. But children's stories during these formal sharing times are often very brief, perhaps because students feel the pressures of time, since teachers are often anxious to give as many students a turn as possible. Many teachers also have a strong preference for "literate" narratives, stories with an explicit beginning, middle, and end. This preference may influence teachers to devalue stories that don't conform to this story-telling formula and may discourage some students from sharing their stories at all. The preference for literate narratives may also explain the tendency of some teachers to take control of children's narratives, often through the use of questions. But not all stories follow the literate story-telling pattern. Sometimes, for example, when we share stories in the context of conversation, certain elements of the narrative (the beginning, setting, or even the ending) may not even be stated explicitly. And good storytellers often deliberately manipulate the story formula for effect.

Michaels and Foster (1985) describe a mixed first- and second-grade class in which students lead the whole-class sharing time while the teacher watches from the edge of the group. Each day the teacher assigns a different student to be the leader. In these student-led groups a variety of sharing styles is encouraged. It's also worth noting that children tell fairly lengthy stories (the longest took eight minutes to recount). Unfortunately, we have also observed student-led sharing groups in which student leaders mimic their teachers and use questioning to take over other children's stories.

Teachers may encourage stories by telling stories themselves—nothing invites a story like another story. Teachers can also encourage story-telling by engaging in informal talk with students throughout the day (see Chapter 8). Children will often share stories with teachers at the beginning or end of the day, between formal lessons, and sometimes even during lessons if teachers are willing (and able) to listen. The stories children volunteer during formal lessons may also allow teachers to link the content of their teaching to children's background knowledge and experience.

Formal story-telling times are another way to encourage the development of children's narrative skills. One third-grade class we know sets aside fifteen minutes each day for students to tell stories. These are usually fictional stories made up by the students themselves or recollections of someone else's stories. Typically, only two or three stories are shared each day. To get story-telling started in the beginning of the year the teacher invited storytellers from the community to the classroom. She also invited parents who liked to tell stories, and she sometimes tells stories herself. This teacher also found that story-telling was a valuable prewriting activity and that transcribed stories could become texts for student reading.

Perhaps the best times for students to tell stories and listen to stories are those informal moments during the day when they talk together in small groups, removed from the pressure of the academic agenda. These times of informal sharing may be especially useful after weekends or vacations or class field trips, when children will want to tell each other about their experiences. And, although the purpose of such talk may not be academic, good teachers will find ways of linking this talk to their lessons, perhaps by helping students choose writing topics or by drawing in some particular aspect of their background experience.

Children's books are an important source of information about formal narrative structures. Teachers who read stories to their students every day show them how stories are put together and in the process encourage them to read stories themselves. The more concerned teachers are about their students' story-telling ability the more they should read to their class each day. It would not be unreasonable to read two or three stories a day to a primary class and to read daily to students in the older grades.

Children also learn about narrative through their writing. What students learn about narrative as they struggle to write and as readers respond to their writing affects both their oral and written language competence.

Teachers are aware that students do not demonstrate equal ability in language. Most children have areas of real strength in language and areas where development is yet to come.

There are times when teachers can help students focus on specific aspects of language so they can achieve their intentions more effectively. Although it isn't our purpose to present an exhaustive list of potential problems or techniques for addressing language problems—there are no fail-proof recipes for helping students learn words or the structure of language—there are a few general principles that can help teachers address language development in the classroom. Teachers can promote vocabulary and syntactic development, or that of any other aspect of language, even particular vocabulary or language structures, by providing students with a rich variety of classroom experiences, by encouraging the use of language for different purposes, and by challenging students to use language to make sense of their lives. These efforts require faith in children's ability to learn language, but there is good reason to believe that such faith is well founded.

7 *Talking and Learning*

A group of girls taking part in a social studies lesson is attempting to discuss prejudice toward other cultures and the problem of arranged marriages for Greek girls. The girls' experience with the concept is quite distant and, consequently, the talk is vague until Helena, a Greek girl in the group, tells the following story:

> 'Cause my mother's got a cousin in America, right? He comes over here to get married. He comes over, we went down to my aunt's to meet him, right? He comes up with this fiancée. Going home I asked my mum, "When did your cousin meet his fiancée? I didn't know he was engaged." She goes, "He met her this morning." I goes, "You mean he met her this morning, she's now engaged to him to be married, and they're going to live together in the States." And she goes, "Yeah." I goes, "That's crazy, your cousin's bloody mad." I really do think he is, because I mean, she met him in the morning and she's engaged to him the same day. I mean, how much could you say in one morning, with everyone else about, when you're meeting all our, you know, all your friends and that, you know, they have quite a bit of a get-together. So how could you really get engaged? You know, she's going to the States and live with him. (Searle, 1988, 27)

Helena draws on her personal experience with her mother's cousin as a way of coming to an understanding of the problems of arranged marriages. The girls have known of arranged marriages only as a cultural concept. Through her talk Helena builds for herself and her friends a context that expands their understanding of what it would mean to live

59

in a society where decisions about marriage are made according to different traditions.

This conversation exemplifies the critical role of talk in learning. Through talk, students are able to bring their experiences and learning together, in essence using language to construct and shape a view of the world. We can see that talk is closely related to how we organize our thinking. This chapter looks at the central importance of talk in classroom learning. We will consider what happens when children use talk to learn and also what happens when we try to teach directly, without allowing for talk. We will then look at some ways to incorporate talk into classroom learning.

The Role of Talk in Learning

Talk plays a crucial role in the reciprocal processes of assimilation and accommodation, which determine how we integrate new knowledge with old knowledge. Using language to learn is a two-way process. Children use language to make sense of new experiences by finding ways to relate them to old knowledge, and they put familiar experiences into words in order to see new patterns in them (Barnes, 1976). As students talk about their experiences, they don't merely add new knowledge: what they already know changes. Because learning requires students to consider what they know as well as what they are learning, we must be aware that what we teach also has the power to change the way students view the world. When students learn they don't just know *more.* As Poplin (1988) says, "Learning isn't additive, it's transformative" (414).

As we talk with children and listen to them talking with each other and with their teachers, we're consistently amazed by what seem to us to be remarkable thinking and problem-solving abilities. The key here is talk. Talking is the principal means by which children show us that they can think and solve problems.

Talk is not only a medium for thinking, it is also an important means by which we learn how to think. From a Vygotskian perspective thinking is an internal dialogue, an internalization of dialogues we've had with others. Our ability to think depends upon the many previous dialogues we have taken part in—we learn to think by participating in dialogues. As a writer learns to anticipate the response of potential audiences, a thinker learns to anticipate the reactions of potential conversational partners. According to Barnes (1976), "In dialogue speakers take up statements that have gone before and develop them: one adds a qualifying condition, another suggests a cause or a result, another negates the whole statement, another reformulates it, and another qualifies one of the objects which it refers to" (90). So the chance to participate in dialogues with peers and teachers will have an important influence on the quality of students' thinking. We may not be able to teach them how to think, but we can offer dialogue as a model of effective thinking and invite them into the process so that they can assimilate effective thinking strategies.

Often when we ask students to use language for learning in the classroom we expect them to express themselves in subject language (such as *import, export; simile, metaphor*). Too often, rather than helping, this language becomes an obstacle that separates students from their everyday language and, in effect, from their everyday knowledge (Barnes, 1976). If students cannot use *their* language to construct *their* own understandings, then developing life-long learning will be that much more difficult.

How Will They Know?

"If I don't tell them, how will they know?" is a question a teacher in one of our graduate education classes asked during a class discussion of the role of the teacher in promoting student learning. The implication is that teaching means giving information, demonstrating skills, covering the curriculum, or sharing content. Schools are structured according to a "transmission" view of learning, and this approach is still deeply embedded in our beliefs about teaching.

For example, we once observed a science lesson in a grade-six class. At the teacher's direction, the students, working in groups of four, put warm water in a 750 ml coke bottle and cold water in a second coke bottle of the same size. They then put blue dye in the bottle of warm water. When they had done this the teacher came around and held the two coke bottles together for them, the warm water on the bottom, cold water on the top. As she did this the blue water (the warm water) flowed from the bottom bottle to the top bottle. The teacher then asked them several direct questions, such as "What's happening here?" "Why?" It was getting close to lunch time and when the students in the group we were observing hesitated, the teacher proceeded to answer her own questions.

This is we think, an example of what Nancy Martin (1976) might call teachers "covering" instead of students "discovering" the curriculum. The teacher told the students what she thought they should have learned from the experiment. But what did these students, denied the opportunity to use their language and experiences to make sense of this science lesson, actually learn? Did they learn anything at all? Would they have felt any need to make the learning make sense for themselves?

It's not that teachers can never tell students anything, as if all school learning needs to be a matter of discovery. Teachers are often in a good position to provide useful explanations, as are other human and print resources. It's just that teachers should realize that there will always be an uneven relationship between what teachers say and what their students hear. The information teachers share with their students is only one part of an internal dialogue going on in students' minds in which they transform what teachers say by combining it with their existing knowledge and experience. This transformation is made effective when these explanations support students' purposes.

When we talk about growth in language we are talking about the ability to use language for an increasing number of purposes. The classroom is a logical setting to consider language growth because language is so fundamental to learning. In the remainder of this chapter we focus on ways to incorporate language use in learning activities.

Helping Students Use Language for Learning

Teachers can't transmit knowledge to their students in the sense that they can give students an understanding of a particular topic. Teachers can, however, create conditions that encourage students to use language to take control of their learning and make their own sense of what happens in the classroom. The following example from a classroom discussion (Berry, 1982, 135–139) shows fifth-grade students actively using what they know to extend their own understanding. These students are doing a science task that requires them to examine a series of twigs and seeds gathered in the neighborhood and arrange them in order from youngest to oldest.

JACK: 'Cause the . . . way of growth . . . that the way they grow.

LIZ: That's the way we *think* they grow.

JACK: Yeah.

SUNNY: Well, that's the closest that we can come to them growing like that . . .

ALTA: We are not sure but it will have to do . . .

JACK: Just wait . . . just [*unintelligible*] they're . . . 'cause remember . . . they get these before they get flowers . . . and they have to get seeds before they get flowers.

SUNNY: No . . . no . . . but . . . no, no, no.

LIZ: Yes they do . . . they have to get seeds before they get flowers.

SUNNY: No.

LIZ: Yeah, sure . . .

(?): Yeah, man . . . freaky man.

SUNNY: Okay, in an apple what do you get first, the apple or the seeds?

TARA: The seeds.

SUNNY: I mean the flowers . . . the apple or the seeds?

JACK: Apples don't have flowers.

SUNNY: Apples tree . . . an apple tree.

LIZ: You get the seeds first.

SUNNY: No you don't . . . 'cause the apples . . . you plant the seed . . . the seed comes from the apple.

LIZ: The seed makes the apple.

ALTA: Yeah.

SUNNY: Noooo.

LIZ: Yes it does . . .

SUNNY: The flower makes the apple . . . and you have to plant the seed . . .

LIZ: Just forget it.

ANGIE: Don't forget it.

JACK: Not to confuse it.

LIZ: You have to plant an apple seed yes . . . then the tree grows you know and it [*the fruit?*] grows . . .

SUNNY: Noooo.

LIZ: Yes!

ALTA: We have a . . . con . . . confume . . .

SUNNY: Confu . . . argument.

ALTA: We have an argument.

SUNNY: I still think that it's . . . because which one comes first? What do you mean?

ALTA: We are not sure if the seed comes first or the flower comes first . . . so that's our argument . . . all right you guys, let's go to the next one.

SUNNY: [*Unintelligible*] Okay, you take your seeds . . . you go outside. Okay . . . the flower comes . . . then you get flowers on it, okay . . . right?

ALTA: Let's go back to this question then.

Here we see students confronting a common concept in science, the life cycle, and trying to work it out in terms of an example taken from their own environment. We see them building understanding, clarifying terminology, and trying to use what they know to make sense of the problem. The problem itself is useful because, although it has an actual answer, it is one that is discussable and encourages deductive reasoning from both observation and scientific understanding. The students recognize that they are having an argument, but they also recognize that this is all right and can listen to another point of view in helping them arrive at the group solution. They believe that they have the resources to reach an answer.

Teachers can follow this teacher's example and encourage students to use language to support their learning by creating a community of learners, allowing students to work in small groups, relating instruction to students' experiences, and, if necessary, influencing student beliefs about teaching and learning.

BUILDING A COMMUNITY OF LEARNERS

In this community of learners, students listen, respond, react, question, challenge, and share, each contributing to the development of the other's learning. The students feel comfortable with each other as they test observations and even as they argue, they recognize that disagreement is a step toward understanding. The development of a classroom community contributes to a zestful learning environment (Hansen, 1987) in which everyone is both a teacher and a learner (Calkins, 1986). The richness of students' talk, and its potential for learning, depends on the development of a learning community; conversely, the learning community is created through talk.

The development of a working community of learners begins with an atmosphere of trust, in which students feel free to speak and express their ideas without fear of correction or ridicule. This kind of community, where students share and learn from each other, is based on mutual support and cooperation. Students learn that everyone has something to share because the teacher demonstrates a belief that each child has something worth sharing (Hansen, 1987).

In order for a cooperative community of learners to flourish, students and their teachers must know each other well. Barnes (1976) suggests that when students know each other well they "can risk inexplicitness, confusion and dead-ends because [they] trust in the tolerance of the others" (109).

Talk flourishes in a community of learners and, in turn, nourishes and sustains the community. Cazden (1988) suggests that activities like sharing time can be justified as much for their contribution to a sense of community as for their contribution to language development. Discussing this reciprocal relationship between talk and the learning community, Rosen and Rosen (1973) conclude that talk "serves not only to teach children about others and how to live with them, but, as it knits groups of children together, it makes new kinds of communication and learning possible" (43). As the community evolves, students are more willing to use language, and the more they use language, the stronger the community will become.

The development of the learning community and students' willingness to use talk to support their learning is also related to the degree to which students are able to take control of their own learning. Once students have something to say and know that someone is interested, the role of talk is guaranteed (Jones, 1988).

By encouraging students to work together, by sharing ideas with them, by listening to them, and by showing faith in their abilities as learners, the teacher can help the students create a community for learning.

GROUPING STUDENTS FOR INSTRUCTION

One way to encourage talk for learning is to have students work in small groups. Small-group discussions allow students to be more honest and directly personal, in contrast to large-group discussions, which encourage more role conformity and posturing.

Small groups are a promising means of encouraging all sorts of talk, including learning talk, but it is not enough just to organize students into groups. As we saw in the science discussion about the twigs, planning must consider several aspects of the activity: "The nature of the task, [students'] familiarity with the subject matter, their confidence in themselves, their sense of what is expected of them, all these affect the quality of the discussion, and these are all open to influence by the teacher" (Barnes, 1976, 71). In the rest of this section we'll discuss some of the ways teachers can influence how students' use talk in small groups.

To be effective, a task must first be interesting to students (Jones, 1988). The immediate focus in the twig example and the opportunity to closely examine the materials contributed to the interest. Because no task, no matter how exciting, will stimulate all students to talk, teachers need to be creative in setting up class activities. The task should also be an open one in which a number of responses are possible. Sorting the twigs encouraged hypothesizing and then required students to call on both their observation and their understanding of what it revealed to support their hypotheses. Jones (1988) suggests that an open-ended task, in which students are asked, for example, to describe instances of pollution they have encountered in their neighborhood or town and to use these ideas to make some general points about the major causes of pollution, is much more likely to be effective than a closed task, in which students are asked to list seven major causes of pollution. In the former case, students are free to speculate and test ideas, since there are no right answers. In the latter case, where the implication is that there are right answers, students may be reluctant to contribute for fear of giving a silly answer and making fools of themselves.

The intended product of small-group discussion will also influence the quality of students' talk. In general, narrowly defined outcomes will almost certainly limit the breadth and depth of discussion. More open-ended outcomes, however, may stimulate lively discussions in which students draw upon their background knowledge and experience to reach a new understanding. Rather than asking students to answer a set of questions in a group, a teacher might provide a list of statements and ask students to sort the list into those with which they agree and those with which they disagree (Jones, 1988). The task of justifying personal decisions leads, as we saw in the twig example, to a more meaningful discussion and a more interesting report. Although a narrowly defined outcome is not conducive to good discussion, no product at all may leave the group frustrated. "It may be necessary to have a product to work towards, a perceived purposeful outcome for the talk, if the talk is to be successful. Talk needs to be about something and needs to be moving somewhere" (Jones, 1988, 105).

Teachers should also consider their own involvement in small groups. First of all, they need to be patient. It may be possible for them to participate effectively in small-group discussions with their students, but this probably can't happen until students gain confidence in their ability to explore ideas independently in small groups and are convinced that this is what their teachers really want from them. Ultimately, teachers will only be able to participate in small-group discussions with students if the task is an open one and if teachers accept that they have as much to learn from their students as students have to learn from them.

Certainly teachers will wish to monitor group activity and will see a value in periodically rearranging groups to provide fresh input and resolve problems in group relations.

RELATING TO STUDENTS' EXPERIENCE

School learning—or any learning—is a matter of making connections between new experiences and what we already know. If we somehow separate school experiences from what our students already know, if we make it impossible for them to use their background knowledge, then real life-long learning will be very difficult, if not impossible. As the students involved in the science task discussed and sorted twigs, they were required to look at their own world from a new perspective. In the best Vygotskian tradition both their own world and the world of school science gained a new connection and a new depth of meaning in the process.

Teachers need to be concerned with using what students already know as a bridge to lead them to new insights. We've heard of one teacher of seven-year-olds who wanted to introduce her children to scientific investigation. To do this she got them to think about what it was they would like to know about people. Finally the class came up with the question, "Do the people with the biggest mouths have the loudest voices?" They then had to develop an investigative strategy. It was easy, they found, to rate the loudest voice, but they had to find a way to measure mouths. They decided that they could measure mouth size by having everyone fill their mouth with water and then spit the water into a cup. The more water, the bigger the mouth. There is a lot of creative scientific thinking in this exercise. The children, in pursuing their personal interests, learned about the scientific method.

The students were also able to keep the experience close to their own understanding because they were able to use their own language to direct the inquiry. Too often we rush to provide word labels to describe processes or to organize learning, when we could let students work with the concept or discover the relationships suggested by the terminology before they have a name for it. Subject terminology, like other kinds of vocabulary, is more easily developed once students have a conceptual framework and are using the concepts themselves.

At times, school experiences may be so far removed from students' experience that teachers may need to help them build up the necessary background knowledge through the use of presentations, films, books, field trips, discussions, and so on. Again, teachers will be best equipped to help students make the necessary connections if they know them well enough to be able to link the learning with their lives.

INFLUENCING STUDENTS' BELIEFS ABOUT
THE VALUE OF TALK

Recently, when a history teacher from the Toronto Public Schools was interviewed on the radio, she said that every year she tried to discuss the Holocaust in her classes and every year at least one student would let her know that this was all very interesting but if it wasn't going to be on the exam they'd just as soon move on.

Teachers aren't the only ones who may need to reexamine their beliefs about human knowledge and teaching and learning. The problem in this example is that the teacher wants her students to see the value in group discussion, but the fact that the school requires examinations and that these examinations are of a certain type tells the students something else.

Jones (1988) found that students have a generally low opinion of the value of small-group discussion as a learning activity. He concluded that one of the major barriers to encouraging students to use talk for learning is the attitude of students themselves toward talk as a learning activity. Similarly, Barnes (1976) states:

> When teachers complain about classes who will not talk they often present this as a moral failing in the pupils: it is more likely that the pupils have learnt from their schooling that their knowledge is irrelevant in a context determined by teachers, examinations, school syllabuses, and so on. (127)

Teachers, especially teachers of older students, may have to be patient when they introduce more talk into their classrooms. It may take a while to convince students of the seriousness of this activity. But students cannot be expected to value talk unless their teachers truly value talk. If teachers encourage students to talk but continue to evaluate them in terms of how well they have "learned" the knowledge teachers have attempted to transmit to them, then students will recognize what's really important to their teachers and, like the students who objected to the Holocaust discussion, will see talk as a relatively meaningless diversion.

Marland (1977) states: *"If a school devotes thought-time to assisting language development, learning in all areas will be helped. If attention is given to language in the content and skill subjects, language development will be assisted powerfully by the context and purpose of those subjects"* (3, his italics). When students don't have the time to talk they will have far fewer opportunities to learn and what they learn will have much less potential to affect their lives.

When they do have time to talk students learn to use language as a tool for thought, for working with others to clarify and communicate ideas, and for becoming independent problem solvers.

8 *Talk-Around-the-Edges*

Our focus so far has been on the classroom as a context for learning. We have looked at the particular kinds of classroom environments that involve children in meaningful talk, at the teacher's role in encouraging and extending that talk, and at ways of using those experiences to develop specific aspects of language use. These chapters have emphasized that talk is at the center of the learning enterprise. In this chapter we wish to focus on a different kind of talk in the classroom. This is talk that while not at the center is just as important in considering the classroom environment as a place for talk. We have come to call this kind of talk "talk-around-the-edges."

When researchers examine classroom language they tend to focus on teacher-controlled instructional talk. There are a variety of good reasons for such a focus. The most obvious is that the greatest bulk of classroom talk is instructional, a reflection of educational assumptions that place a premium on teacher-directed activity and "on-task" behavior. Students are most often asked to talk in order to be evaluated and corrected. Other verbal contributions may be seen as distracting or ill informed.

We have a different view of student talk. In a detailed look at classroom talk, Mehan (1979) confirmed the central role of the teacher in organizing talk but also noted an undercurrent of student talk that, at times, became a part of the ongoing discourse. Some of this talk could be disruptive, but some of it was encouraged and used by the teacher to further pedagogic and social goals. In this chapter we want to look at the nature and value of what we call talk-around-the-edges, particularly when this talk is between teachers and students.

71

What Is Talk-Around-the-Edges?

For our awareness of the value of talk-around-the-edges we have to thank one teacher in a research project. Observing this teacher over several days we were struck by her manner of engaging students as they entered the classroom, as they got their jackets when leaving the classroom for recess or after dismissal, and in breaks between and even during lessons. Regularly the teacher hovered near the coat hooks and chatted with the students about their day, about what was going on in their lives outside school, and about their families. Students responded freely and easily. Here is a sample of this teacher's interactions with her students as they got ready for recess.

MELISSA: [*Referring to a friend's socks*] I like those socks.
TEACHER: Aren't they pretty socks? You've pretty socks too.
MELISSA: Yes, I like them.
TEACHER: All sorts of fanciness on the socks.
MELISSA: They're at the BiWay [*a local discount store*]. But not on, on this street or Thornhill. But they're on this, my old street, where we used to live.
TEACHER: I see.
MELISSA: At the BiWay. There's very cheap.
TEACHER: Is it in Willowdale?
MELISSA: On [*unintelligible*] street.
TEACHER: Oh.
MELISSA: There's elastic so I can roll them.
TEACHER: Yes, they look good that way.
MELISSA: Like this? Or that?
TEACHER: I like them rolled over. What do you like?
MELISSA: I like it down.

This conversation is neither spectacular nor profound, but its implications are important for this teacher's work with her children. Through it she establishes herself as a listener and friend; the child gets an opportunity to share her life and preferences and to interact with the teacher on an equal footing. But this isn't *just* talk. In order to communicate as an equal Melissa must develop her linguistic resources to focus her meaning clearly. She is sharing what she knows and what she likes, information unknown to the teacher. To make it known she must use language carefully and precisely. The challenge to communicate provides the pressure she needs to expand and develop her language. Rosen and Rosen (1973) see this pressure as crucial for language development and encourage teachers to seek out just such situations to extend students' talk.

> Children have available much more linguistic competence than usually finds its way into their speech. We need to create those situations which exert the greatest pressure on them to use their latent resources, to provide those experiences which urge them towards the widest range of language use. (64)

When we looked closely at other teachers we could find instances when they too engaged in talk-around-the-edges, and we became further convinced of its importance in encouraging language growth.

In another cloakroom conversation involving Melissa and several other children we can see how language is stretched in order to make meaning.

MELISSA: Today, ah, today's not my day. Today when I . . . be-fore I went out . . . I kissed my Mom before I went out and I . . . my glasses were on the floor and I stepped on them.

TEACHER: Oh.

MELISSA: And the glasses fell out.

TEACHER: Oh dear.

MELISSA: But she said it's okay. At least she didn't, at least I didn't get in trouble.

TEACHER: Oh, I'm glad. Melissa, you're ready quickly.

KAREN: Today's my day.

MILES: Can we ah, I would like to do that, ah for, ah, I want to see how I grow up . . . now . . . again.

TEACHER: The measuring?

MILES: Yeah.

TEACHER: Oh we did it just a few weeks ago. We'll wait now till school's nearly over. Then we'll measure you again.

MARK: Can we . . . ?

MILES: When?

TEACHER: In June.

MILES: June. That's good.

MARK: Mrs. P. Um . . . did . . . can I get myself measured? I want to see if I'm growing any since we put the tape.

TEACHER: Well you could do that for yourself sometime just for fun. But we'll measure everybody in June and put up new cards.

MARK: That's what I said. That's what I did this morning when I was waiting at the chalkboard. I just said let me see how much I, if I growed a little bit. And I did.

There is a rambling nature to this sort of conversation that allows new interests and concerns to emerge. In their discussion the students had to reorient the conversation and identify an event they wished to return to. This loose structure invites students to bring in their immediate interests.

Talk-Around-the-Edges and Language Development

The following conversation took place in another classroom at the beginning of class, as children came in and moved to the hamster cage to look at the new litter. In this instance, the hamsters prompted interested talk that involved the teacher. Another student's arrival shifted the focus. The situation provided the children with an opportunity to express their personal reactions and observations, but it also demanded that they shape these personal views into a socially understandable form. In the process, the students struggled with their own language resources.

SYLVESTER: There are six or seven babies all curled up . . . in one spot.

TEACHER: They're sleeping together.

ARCHIBALD: They're piled up on each other.

TEACHER: I guess that's to keep cozy and warm. Do you think that they need to keep themselves warm?

WILLIAM: There's a black one and a brown [*inaudible*].

ARCHIBALD: And [*inaudible*].

TEACHER: I didn't realize that . . . How many black ones are there?

ARCHIBALD: One, two, three. Angus, Angus you [*inaudible*].

WILLIAM: And the mother, baby . . . baby . . . the mother had a . . .

TEACHER: Another litter?

WILLIAM: Yeah.

TEACHER: You're right. I guess there's been one from every litter hasn't there?

STUDENTS: [*Inaudible background conversation and laughing*]

TEACHER: Can you save that till news time? I'd like to see you join . . .

STEVEN: [*Inaudible*] big box. I couldn't bring to school. Mom said.

TEACHER: Your Mom said?

STEVEN: Yeah.

TEACHER: Where did you find the caterpillar?

JOSHUA: Under a roof, under where people [*inaudible*].

ARCHIBALD: . . . side of the road?

STEVEN: Yeah . . . He was digging up some weeds and all of a sudden the caterpillar dropped down [*inaudible*].

STEVEN: Black and blue . . .

ARCHIBALD: It was . . . you found somewhere in the road?

This conversation may appear poorly developed and even irrelevant. In it, however, we can see the process of language learning at work. The children struggle to clarify their focus ("and the mother, baby . . . baby . . . the mother had a . . . "), to orient their listeners to the topic, to communicate information, to recreate experience ("He was digging up some weeds and all of a sudden the caterpillar dropped down"). Their vocabulary is stretched ("under a roof, under where people"), they ask questions, organize events in sequence, make meaning explicit, and learn to handle the give-and-take of conversation. Certainly, as in most people's conversations, they are not always successful. However, their failure is greeted not as in a language lesson with evaluation and instruction but with support and requests for clarification, as in a normal conversation. Indeed, one of the features of talk-around-the-edges is that teachers are not aware of the language learning in progress.

In these situations teachers are much more apt to respond like any authentic audience. The topics introduced by the students may be new to the teachers, so that students get to speak in the role of expert. The teachers focus on the meaning and intent of the conversation, and their response confirms the communication or clarifies the communication difficulty. Other students who may have heard the story or have shared the experience serve to elaborate, extend, or challenge what has been said. In this way, students explore language and its possibilities.

We also noticed talk-around-the-edges in situations similar to those noted by Mehan in which students used breaks in the lessons to relate the topic to their own interests. This talk oozed into instructional events when students extended or diverted the topic, or made personal responses where teachers may not have expected them. In the following examples, students interrupt individual reading sessions. The reading material is a reading program with a controlled vocabulary. The text is simple and lifeless. Nevertheless, the conversational diversions illustrate how students enrich the language and demonstrate strategies for comprehension that will serve them well as readers.

TEACHER: All right, get some cards, what do the first three say?

SANDY: Sat . . . is . . . fied. Satisfied.

TEACHER: What was the story about?

SANDY: Um, Mrs. Brent couldn't sleep 'cause, um, the next door neighbor snored so loud, and kept her all awake.

TEACHER: So what did they do?

SANDY: Um, she called the police, and the police closed the window in her bedroom, and his bedroom, and the kids' bedroom, and he can sleep in his own bedroom.

TEACHER: And everybody was . . . ?

SANDY: Satisfied.

TEACHER: [*Laughs*] Right. That's a problem when you're snoring. It disturbs the people next door, doesn't it?

SANDY: My dad snores if he falls asleep on the couch and my mom has to hit him with the pillow to get up and go into the bedroom.

TEACHER: People who snore don't believe they do either, do they? They don't hear themselves. [*Laughs*]

SANDY: Yeah. [*Laughs*]

TEACHER: All right. You finish that and I'll check the work.

In this first example it is the teacher who moves away from the text to comment on the problem with snoring. This may appear as an irrelevant diversion, a short, controlled break, but, in fact, it demonstrates how a reader reacts to a text and relates it to personal experience. The student picks up from the teacher with a personal account of her dad's snoring, which demonstrates an understanding of the basic situation in the story. The teacher could ask whether Sandy under-

stood the story, but the answer would be a simple yes or no.
In this situation the teacher has a better sense of Sandy's
comprehension, and Sandy has had the opportunity to
recount her own experience.

The teacher's practice of mixing personal observations with
the reading encouraged the students to initiate their own
diversions, as in the following excerpt taken from a reading
lesson in which Jason and Marshall read aloud from a basal
reader.

JASON: [*Reading*] "Dad's job is to fix the box. Ned's job is to
cut, to cut six big logs."
TEACHER: Excellent, okay.
JASON: Must be grounded. [*Laughs*] If somebody got
grounded they wouldn't be doing that, if nobody
got grounded they wouldn't be doing that, you have to
cut six blocks.
TEACHER: You think that would be a punishment, do you? Oh
well, maybe he likes doing that. All right, Marshall? [*Marshall begins reading.*]

Jason's comment is remarkable evidence of his behavior as
an active reader. The story he is reading is a contrived tale
using controlled vocabulary, yet Jason seeks an underlying
rationale behind the events, calling on his experience of work
as punishment to speculate about why Ned is doing this
work with his dad. This is a diversion but it is also the behavior of a good reader.

In each case, the break has allowed students to enter and
divert the instruction in order to interact with the text
in a way that is meaningful in their own lives. In the first
excerpt, the teacher interrupts to offer a comment on snoring. The student takes the opportunity to add a personal
experience the reading suggests to her. In the second, the
teacher has signaled the end of a sequence by saying,
"Excellent, okay," but before the teacher signals a move forward Jason enters with his own interpretation. Throughout,
the teacher's control of the diversion is clear. In the first
excerpt she, in fact, initiates the diversion. What is more
important, from the teacher's perspective she is able to signal an end to the diversion with the words "all right" and
indicate the next instructional direction. In a sense, however,
we can see that, whereas the instruction is aimed at helping

the children "to read," the diversions are fulfilling the equally valuable task of helping the children "to become readers" by learning that readers interact with text in order to make it make sense for them.

In another classroom children are reporting the day's news during class news time. One item refers to crossing the border into the United States, a familiar experience for many Toronto-area school children.

STUDENT: When you're going to the United States you also have this big bridge you could go across.

TEACHER: Why?

STUDENT: That's the border because, so you could get to the United States.

TEACHER: Often you have to go across a bridge.

JEREMY: You have to bring your driver's license and I forget the other thing.

TEACHER: Does anyone know what?

STUDENT: Credit card!

TEACHER: I don't think . . .

STUDENT: Your ID.

TEACHER: Identification . . . you need something. What do you have to take for identification if you want to go to another country?

STUDENT: Like on a plane you have to.

JEREMY: Your . . . your birth . . .

TEACHER: That's one thing, birth certificate, and if you're going farther away than the United States sometimes you have to get what we call a passport, then take that with you. It has a picture of you in it too. All your information. Yes? Larry?

LARRY: You'll have to get a credit card so you can get United States money.

TEACHER: Well, sometimes you can go to the bank and get United States money before you go. Some people take a credit card but some people do both.

JEREMY: He drives a car. That's why he had to bring his license.

STUDENT: What kind of car?

TEACHER: Okay . . .

JEREMY: He drives my dad's.

TEACHER: Okay Mark, did you have something you wanted to ask Jeremy?

A student has diverted Jeremy from his account of his brother's trip, and the children begin to share what they know about crossing borders. It is apparent that the teacher has encouraged this diversion, letting the class talk and introducing the concept of a passport. This digression allows the students to draw on their own knowledge to expand and support their learning. They display considerable evidence of their own thinking.

These diversions give teachers the opportunity to see what their students know and what they are learning, and give students the opportunity to use their language to support their learning. Their responses reflect their need to justify their assertions, such as Jeremy's explanation of why his brother needed his driver's license or Larry's explanation of why a credit card is needed. The students also seem to work hard to retrieve specific information. We can see them stretching their vocabulary by putting their own experience into words. When the teacher senses that the request for information about the car will lead the talk into a less speculative mode, she signals an end to the episode. It turns out that these apparent diversions aren't really diversions at all. They are instead central to the topic and to the learning that is at the heart of classroom activity. Talk-around-the-edges contributes to the learning, in part, by allowing students to introduce their own experience and knowledge of the world into the context of learning.

Talk-Around-the-Edges and Indirect Teaching

In talk-around-the-edges teachers have less control of the topic. Consequently, students find themselves in the role of the expert, struggling to share their expertise. The feedback they receive tends to be related to their success in making their meaning clear. This talk also serves to help students bring learning and experience together. If students are to integrate their learning into their emerging understanding, it serves teachers well to listen to the personal experiences that are invoked by classroom activities.

By its very nature, talk-around-the-edges cannot be scheduled into classroom time. It is possible, however, to create an environment in which students feel that they can share their experience. Finding occasions within daily routines for the personal chat that invites extended personal talk is one practice that deserves encouragement. Teacher-initiated diversions also invite student diversions by modeling an appropriate personal response and by softening the boundaries of instructional talk to allow space for talk-around-the-edges. Teachers' willingness to encourage or tolerate talk-around-the-edges is closely related to their beliefs about teaching and learning and their respect for what students have to say. It is also possible to listen for the diversions students initiate and to seek out the logic and connections students are making. Not every diversion is profitable, and we can never be sure that we have opened up or closed down talk at the right time. Nevertheless, by being more open, we can increase the likelihood of successful extended discourse that will lead students to develop the language and interaction skills we are attempting to encourage.

The teachers in our examples did not view this talk as a part of language development and were to a large extent unaware of it. But they were aware that they were using talk to personalize the classroom or to get students ready to work. This should remind us of a basic irony in teaching language: we teach language best when we aren't aware that we are doing it.

The following session between a teacher and a young student (for which we are indebted to Annette Gaskin), demonstrates this irony strikingly. Tahlia is a seven-year-old girl from an East-Indian family. She had been sent to an "English-as-a-second-language" teacher because her classroom teacher had trouble following her train of thought. Tahlia, the teacher said, seemed to stray off topic, made inappropriate responses to questions, and seemed to have trouble labeling. It was felt that a recent prolonged visit to her family in India might have confused her language patterns. The ESL teacher determined that Tahlia's English was adequate but continued to work with her to help her with labeling and her difficulty in responding to questions.

In this session, the teacher had set up a toy farm on a table to provide a context for talk relating to farm life. Prior to the planned interaction, however, the teacher greeted Tahlia with a hug, which triggered the following exchange.

TAHLIA: My grandmother hugs like that and my dad so . . . I like that. We . . .
TEACHER: Is that right?

TAHLIA: My dad doesn't like to hug.

TEACHER: Doesn't he?

TAHLIA: No, he only likes to hug us.

TEACHER: Oh. Well, when you see your grandmother you'll be so happy. How is she going to get here from India?

TAHLIA: Umm . . . by plane.

TEACHER: Oh . . . who's going to pick her up?

TAHLIA: We are . . . like, and uh, my Mom said that we are gonna have a party.

TEACHER: Won't that be exciting?

TAHLIA: Yes . . . in our house.

TEACHER: Have you, have you ever been to the airport before?

TAHLIA: Yeah, I've been lots of times.

TEACHER: Why are you dressed up today?

TAHLIA: I dunno. My mom told me it's hot so I was gonna wear my pants, but I'll celebrate . . . wear a dress.

This exchange is a clear example of talk-around-the-edges. It certainly achieves its primary function of establishing a relationship between the teacher and child, setting a climate for continuing language exchanges. But we also need to look at Tahlia's performance in relation to what the teachers have said about her language. She initiates a discussion that makes good sense in which she shares information about her family. She answers seven questions directed at her by the teacher in a manner that illustrates that she clearly understands the nature and form of the questions. Her language in most answers is beyond the minimum required to answer and, in fact, in most of her responses she extends and adds information. In this conversational context she shares information that is close to her, important to her, and real to her, and her answers reflect her interest and personal expertise. The teacher is attentive and allows Tahlia ample opportunity to share her news.

The teacher then moved the conversation into the "formal" part of the lesson by leading Tahlia over to the table where the toy farm was set up. The lesson focused on the observed need to improve Tahlia's ability to label things.

TEACHER: Oh . . . Tahlia, look around . . . what do you see here that we might be talking about today . . . can you see anything on the table that might give you a hint?

TAHLIA: A farm!

TEACHER: That's right! Have you ever been to a farm before?

TAHLIA: Yeah . . . in a trip . . . was with . . . the teacher.

TEACHER: What kind of animals did you see on the farm?

TAHLIA: Oh . . . I think chick . . . ens, ducks and pigs and cows and some flowers.

TEACHER: What other animals did you see though?

TAHLIA: Ah . . . I think . . . a horse and a cow, pigs, chickens, ducks . . . a cat, dog . . . that's it.

TEACHER: All right . . . What do you call this great big building . . . that the animals live in?

TAHLIA: Farm.

TEACHER: Well the great big, the place where the animals stay is called a farm.

TAHLIA: Barn!

TEACHER: Very good! Can you open up the barn and see what's inside?

TAHLIA: Oh, I love building [*unintelligible*].

TEACHER: Okay, you, do you think you can take some of those things out and tell me about them when you take them out?

TAHLIA: Okay . . . these are the friends. This . . . whoops . . . this is the horse, this the cow, and this is the sh . . . eep, and this is, is . . . a pig.

TEACHER: Right.

TAHLIA: What is this? . . . Oh boy! . . . This is the truck and this is . . . I forgot.

TEACHER: What did you call this?

TAHLIA: A truck?

TEACHER: It's not exactly a truck. The farmer uses it for different things. Sometime he uses . . .

TAHLIA: To build a [*unintelligible*].

TEACHER: Pardon me?

TAHLIA: To make seed grow up.

TEACHER: Seed? That's right. Sometimes he takes it into the field and plants the seed, but what's this thing called . . . do you remember?

TAHLIA: Tractor!

TEACHER: Very good, see?

The language in this excerpt contrasts sharply with the earlier exchange. The language of labeling makes few demands on Tahlia's linguistic repertoire, and her talk is far simpler than in the earlier exchanges in the greeting section.

Tahlia shows very little difficulty in labeling items that are somewhat, but not completely, a part of her experience. It is clear that she would like to end the lesson and get on with playing. We have to wonder whether such a limited focus is the best way to help Tahlia develop her ability to make meaningful extended discourse. The irony is apparent. When the teacher was talking with Tahlia, she drew out extended, coherent discourse and gave her ample opportunity to answer questions with meaningful content. When the teacher was teaching language the talk was simpler and less extended, and the answers focused on word selection over meaning. We would argue that the teaching was more effective in the talk-around-the-edges, and that in this kind of conversation Tahlia would most likely develop the language patterns her teachers feared she had lost.

In planning an environment for purposeful talk, we must remember that language is alive at all times in the classroom. Talk that may appear to be peripheral to the instructional intent of the teacher may in fact provide students with a welcome chance to engage in extended talk about areas of personal knowledge and interest and to expand their language repertoires. The teacher, as an interested listener and conversational partner, becomes a different kind of audience in these exchanges. By purposefully including talk-around-the-edges in planning the classroom environment, teachers will find that the entire climate for talk is improved.

9   *Teachers as Reflective Practitioners*

Assessment is an integral part of teaching. It enables us to describe students' development, plan our lessons, and adapt our instruction as needed. In order to develop conditions favorable to language learning, teachers must continually assess children's language and the possible effects of the learning environment, including their lessons, on children's language use.

The assessment of students' language, like our instructional practices, is rooted in our beliefs about language teaching and learning. When language is viewed as a sequence of discrete skills, students' competence is assessed by administering formal and informal tests before and after instruction. These tests are used to determine the direction of teaching and to evaluate its effects.

Although we also see assessment as a means of monitoring students' language use and adapting instruction, from our more holistic perspective assessment is inextricably linked to instruction and learning, not something that merely precedes or follows it. Effective language teachers constantly evaluate and modify their instruction as they observe and interact with their students. Assessment is part of everything that we've discussed so far, and we've placed these chapters toward the end of the book in part to emphasize this point.

In this chapter and the following two chapters we'll outline an observational approach to assessing students' language, look at the effects of language instruction, and examine the assumptions that underlie language instruction in our classrooms. We'll begin by arguing that teachers do more than simply assess language. As reflective practitioners or researchers, they study children's language, how children learn language, and how they as teachers can influence children's language development. And as researchers their focus is on describing students' language ability—what they *can do*—since this is the foundation upon which teachers can build.

Teachers as Researchers

Teaching isn't something we learn to do once and for all. Teachers are always learning to teach; we are always in the process of becoming teachers. But learning to teach—in this case, learning to teach language—isn't a matter of accumulating more programs, kits, or clever ideas, moving from one bandwagon to another, or just keeping up with the latest literature. Although teachers can learn to teach, no one, including researchers or the publishers of kits and materials, can tell them *precisely* what to do in their classrooms. Angela Jaggar (1989) expresses a similar sentiment when she says:

> No specific theory or research study or curriculum guide can prescribe what is appropriate for individual students in a particular classroom. Only teachers can make those decisions. *Formal theories and the research on which they are based are descriptive, not prescriptive; they provide possibilities, not formulas for practice.* (74, emphasis added)

Teachers learn how to teach by carefully observing students in their classrooms and in other settings and then stepping back and reflecting on what they've observed. This combination of observation and informed reflection becomes inquiry, and the teachers become researchers. As researchers, teachers are learners and, like other learners, they learn by doing, in this case by teaching (Jaggar, 1989). Teachers can, and should, seek guidance from the literature and other resources, but it's up to them to make sense of these resources in terms of their own situation and personal experiences.

Like other researchers teachers begin with questions to be answered: "For what purposes do my students use language?" "What sense does Margaret make of 'why' questions?" "What is the effect of my presence on small-group talk?" To answer these and other questions about classroom language or language instruction, teachers must observe students in a range of settings. Teachers may eavesdrop on students as they play on the playground or talk in small groups in the classroom ("Does Ashley, who rarely talks in class, talk to her friends on the playground?"). Or they may carefully attend to the language that is part of their own interactions with students ("Do I dominate conversations with students? What kinds of questions do I ask?"). The key here is that teachers observe students as students use language to fulfill their *own* intentions, not somebody else's that have been contrived for purposes of assessment.

It is essential that teachers make occasional notes to document what they have observed, including examples of student language that relate to their questions. Teachers might, for instance, record examples of settings in which a student uses language successfully and settings in which she does not. A student may use language for problem solving in small group discussions but not in whole-class discussions. Or a teacher may note differences in a student's language in formal and informal situations (perhaps Theresa is able to narrate a story to a small group of friends but not to adults).

Some teachers keep research logs or teaching diaries to record interesting examples of children's language and their impressions about the language-learning environment. Teachers may use a tape recorder to record students' language, which they can play back, for example, in the car on the way to and from school. Since it's impossible to observe all of the students in the class at once, some teachers pick out two or three students to observe each day. One teacher we know puts the names of three students on separate 4" x 6" cards. Throughout the day she then makes a special effort to focus on the performance (reading, writing, math, *and* oral language) of these students in class, on the playground, in the lunchroom, and in the halls. In more remarkable cases, she may focus on only one student for the day. But even though she's focusing on only a few students each day, she's still alert to the other children in her class and may record interesting observations about them too ("Today Brad was much more active in our small-group social studies discussion. Brad's friend, Thomas, who usually dominates this group's discussions, was absent today. Perhaps I should move Brad to another group when Thomas returns").

This all sounds very time-consuming and distracting, but it needn't be. Teachers who move away from teacher-centered classrooms and create frequent opportunities for their students to use language provide themselves with opportunities to observe and make notes. When students have time to talk, teachers have time to listen.

Learning to be a good observer of children is a skill that must be developed over a period of time. But in general, teachers become researchers more by adopting an inquiring stance or attitude toward teaching and learning than by receiving special training, although such training may be helpful. As Britton (1987) notes, "If research is seen primarily as a process of discovery, then the day-to-day work of a teacher comes under the term *teachers as researchers....* This requires that every lesson should be for the teacher an inquiry, some further discovery, a quiet form of research" (15). According to this viewpoint, research is a fundamental part of teaching. Although all research begins with a question to be answered, in classroom research old questions generate new questions, so there will always be a sense in which the research is never finished (Odell, 1989).

Teachers who adopt the questioning, inquiring stance of a researcher may never be the same. Teachers who observe their students as they use language and respond to language instruction will increase their understanding of language and language learning and their knowledge of students—all of which will make them better teachers. Teachers who study language may also increase their confidence in their students and in their power to teach (Milz, 1989). And what and how they teach may change. Atwell (1987) concluded that the teachers in her school who studied students' writing dramatically altered their approach to teaching writing. Similar effects can be expected for teachers who study oral language.

Dialogue is essential for professional development (Jaggar, 1989). Teachers will learn the most when they have opportunities to talk about what they observe in their classes. Learning is a social process and teachers, like students, need opportunities to engage in social dialogue with their colleagues.

The questions teachers ask and how they go about studying language and language learning are functions of their beliefs about the nature of language and language learning and about the abilities of their students. The effect of teachers' beliefs about students on assessment is equally significant.

Focusing on Students' Abilities

While we were working on this book, Dudley-Marling suffered through another Super Bowl loss by his beloved Denver Broncos, their third in four years. As a result, the Broncos were ridiculed in the newspapers and sports magazines for their failures, while their accomplishments (many teams have *never* been to a Super Bowl) were ignored. Sometimes we look at children with this same sort of tunnel vision—seeing them for what they don't do or haven't done (live up to our expectations) while overlooking their marvelous achievements.

Consider the following example. When three-year-old Ian's father lifted him over the back of a chair and sat him in it, Ian said, "That's like a merry-go-up." What should we make of "merry-go-up?" Should we view it as a language error? After all, there is no such word as "merry-go-up." Or should we see it as an example of the cute utterances by children that make adults laugh? Or should we see "merry-go-up" as evidence of children's remarkable creativity and language ability? How we finally interpret children's language is a function of our perceptions of their ability.

When we doubt children's ability, when we perceive them in terms of problems, skill deficits, or disabilities, we are more likely to look for evidence of what's wrong with them and less inclined to look for evidence of what they can do. In Chapter 2 we included an example of a child who described a picture by saying he was skating "*in* the Mill Pond." The teacher concluded that the student's language was ambiguous, that he had a fundamental difficulty in being explicit, a condition she needed to "fix." This conclusion was influenced, at least in part, by her belief that the student had a language problem.

Chris Dudley-Marling, a speech pathologist, tells a similar story. Chris visited a preschool program to observe a girl (we'll call her Gloria) who would be attending Chris's school the next fall. The speech pathologist who was working with Gloria at the time believed that Gloria suffered from "echolalia," the tendency to repeat what she hears. To demonstrate

Gloria's "problem," the speech pathologist held a bowl of cereal up in front of her, high enough so that the girl couldn't see what was in the bowl, and asked Gloria, "What is it?" Gloria responded, "What is it?" The speech pathologist repeated the question with a similar result. Apparently she had been able to demonstrate the girl's echolalia. Or had she? When Chris told this story, she said that, based on various nonverbal cues, she didn't hear echolalia. She heard a girl who asked, "What is it?" because she was curious about what was in the bowl. We think it's likely that the speech pathologist's assessment decision—that this sample of the girl's speech was echolalic—was influenced by her prior beliefs.

What we see in our students is a function of the questions we ask; the questions we ask are, in turn, affected by our beliefs about the collective and individual abilities of our students as language users and language learners. Even Piaget would appear to have underestimated children's ability in view of the questions he asked (or didn't ask) (see Donaldson, 1978). If we presume that a child or a group of children is limited in their language ability we may look for evidence of problems and easily accept such evidence when we find it. If we trust children's ability to learn, however, we will look for evidence of their ability and question evidence to the contrary.

And there's plenty of evidence that our students can and do learn. Virtually all the students in our classrooms, even those who seem to have language problems, know a great deal about language. They know thousands of words and complex rules for ordering words to express their ideas. They also know how to use these rules appropriately in various communicative settings. And, of course, they know a lot about the world in which they live. Our task as teachers is to try to find out what our students *do* know about language and how they use language to fulfill their needs.

Seeing students in terms of abilities and not problems may have a dramatic effect on how we interpret their language behavior. When we are confronted with what seem to be strange comments (for example, Erin, a second grader, interjects during a class discussion about dinosaurs, "My dad took us to New York last year") we may probe the logic behind this language and, more often than not, we will find it. (It turned out that while Erin's family was in New York they visited the Museum of Natural History where she saw dinosaurs.) We may also begin to see unconventional or nonstandard language as evidence of growth and not as errors. We will recognize that children who overgeneralize past tense markers (runned, bleeded) aren't (just) making mistakes; they're testing sophisticated hypotheses about how language works. We will see that students who don't talk in complete sentences don't necessarily have a problem—they may just be doing what the rest of us do. If someone asks us what we're carrying under our arm, we'll likely respond, "a book," or "magazine," and not, "I'm carrying a magazine under my arm." Similarly, we may understand that sometimes dysfluency is a harbinger of growth and that children may temporarily lose control over some aspects of language as they gain control over others. In sum, we'll see students as language learners and not as a collection of problems, skill deficits, or disabilities.

Assessment serves instruction by continually informing teachers both about the progress of their students' language development and about the effect their language teaching has on that development. Good assessment begins with an inquiring stance and a belief in the ability of children. Children are brilliant language learners. Our needs and theirs are best served when we recognize this.

10 *Assessing Student Language*

In this chapter we'll begin by discussing how we would go about assessing the language of individual students. Then we'll examine the role talk can play as a "window into student learning." We'll conclude with a discussion of the effects of the instructional environment on students' language.

Does It Work?

The most common way to assess students' language, especially if we suspect that there is a problem, is to administer a test. Language tests usually yield some measure of students' language abilities in one or more areas (syntax, receptive and expressive vocabulary, and so on) by comparing the performance of individual students to group norms. The basic question we ask when we adopt this approach to assessment is "How much language do students have" (in comparison to other students the same age)? It's as if we could slide a dipstick into children's "language receptacle" and measure the amount of language in it. Inevitably, this kind of assessment focuses language instruction on the skills or abilities children don't have because it refers us to a predetermined sequence of language abilities they are supposed to have.

From our perspective, "How much language do they know?" isn't a very interesting question. This approach to assessment limits our scope and narrows instruction to teaching skills that students don't have *simply because they don't have them,* without reference to whether they want them or need them. It's like teaching someone to bowl just because they don't know how, not because they need or want to learn to bowl. Some readers might protest that this isn't a fair comparison. After all, everyone needs to learn language and conventional language forms at that. This is true to an extent. But children and adults don't learn language merely for the sake of learning it. They learn language for some purpose, as a tool for getting things done. So language assessment must focus on the language user's intentions. The question isn't "What does she know about language?" or "Does he know anything about language?" but, rather, *"How do students use language to fulfill their needs?"*

When the purpose of language is communication, the effectiveness of a person's language can only be determined by examining its effect on the audience. If a speaker seeks to persuade, is the audience persuaded? Or, if someone tries to give directions, can the listener follow them? (Of course, the listener also has some responsibility here.) The only valid test of language use is: Does it work? If it doesn't work, then we can ask why.

Sometimes this principle is ignored and children's language is judged by comparing it to arbitrary adult standards (he doesn't speak in "complete" sentences or she doesn't use standard English) and not according to whether or not it works. For purposes of illustration, let's consider children's narratives. We know from our own experience and from the research literature that many teachers prefer student stories that are "literate"—with a clearly marked beginning, middle, and end—like the stories in children's books (Michaels, 1981; Michaels and Foster, 1985). But in a study of student-led sharing groups, Michaels and Foster (1985) used the commonsense criterion of audience response to differentiate successful and unsuccessful sharing turns. A successful turn held the audience's attention. An unsuccessful turn didn't. Michaels and Foster found that successful story-telling had more to do with the ability of the storyteller to pay attention to and capitalize on audience reactions and monitor audience cues and feedback than the storyteller's adherence to a literate narrative formula. In fact, Michaels and Foster found both successful and unsuccessful turns that had clear beginnings, middles, and ends.

So the important question to ask about children's stories focuses not on their structure but on the response of the audience. This notion generalizes to all aspects of language. Ultimately, we care more about function and less about form. We aren't saying that form isn't important. It is. But it's important only insofar as it affects function. If children's narratives aren't successful (they don't hold the audience's attention), then questions about the structure of children's stories become more interesting. A storyteller's difficulty with the code (that is, syntax) may make it very difficult for the audience to make sense of the story. Or the story may fail because the audience prefers formal standard English. But, of course, a problem with form isn't the only reason a storyteller may fail. Referring to the research of Michaels and Foster (1985), we would also ask questions about the ability of the storyteller to read and respond to audience cues.

Teachers assess students' language by asking questions that will help them to plan, adapt, and evaluate their language instruction. But the precise questions that individual teachers ask is a matter of professional choice, which is based on the unique interaction of their needs as teachers, the needs of their students, and the physical, social, and cultural environment in which they teach. It would be presumptuous of us to offer a definitive list of questions for teachers to follow. Teachers must decide this for themselves. But we can offer some guidelines for assessing children's language. (We would add that when teachers suspect a problem with students' speech and language development they should also consult with a speech-language pathologist.)

First of all, any question that can be answered with a simple yes or no usually won't be very helpful. Questions like "Does he know anything about language?" aren't useful since it's hard to imagine a child in school who doesn't already know a lot about language. And questions like "Can he tell a story?" or "Is she able to use language to direct others?" can't really be answered with a simple yes or no, since the answer to these questions must always be qualified with reference to the context. Teachers sometimes talk about students who can't listen or can't follow directions, for example. But it's unlikely that we could find a student who never listens or never follows instructions. We would do better to try to describe the conditions under which students listen or follow instructions (or tell a story) and those in which they do not. If Sherry is able to carry out complex instructions when she is alone with her teacher, but she rarely follows through when there is a class full of children, the problem may not be that Sherry doesn't understand her teacher's directions or that she easily forgets them. It may just be that Sherry is easily distracted by her friends while she attempts to carry them out.

Context is always a factor in language use so we must be alert to its effects. We know an eight-year-old boy whose language, according to his teacher, was almost totally incomprehensible. When she looked more closely, however, she found that his language use was much more effective when he interacted with younger children, whose language development was similar to his. So he wasn't *always* difficult to understand, only in some contexts. Even structural complexity and vocabulary are affected by contextual factors such as interest, purpose, audience, and so on. Therefore, it's important to observe children's language in as many contexts as possible, especially when we suspect there is a problem. Even then, we should be cautious about generalizing our observations to settings we have not observed.

Similarly, it's best to think in terms of *does* or *doesn't* or even *won't* instead of *can't* when describing students' language: "He doesn't use regular past tense" not "He can't use regular past tense." *Can't* implies that a child is unable to do something, but we can't know that (*can't*, in this case, is appropriate). We only know what children do and when they do it.

The ultimate goal of language learners (and the language teacher) is to increase the range of purposes for which they can use language and the settings in which they can use language. Therefore, teachers will want to identify the various purposes for which their students do use language and the contexts in which they fulfill these purposes, especially in cases where students seem to be struggling with language. How and when does the student use language to tell stories? To question? To talk about personal experiences? To imagine? To solve problems? Of course, when we examine this range of purposes, we're evaluating our curriculum as much as we are students' language. If students don't use language to solve problems, we need to ask ourselves whether we've provided opportunities for students to solve problems. We'll say more about this later.

When teachers discover situations in which students' language breaks down, when it isn't effective, they'll want to get a sense of what the problem is. Imagine we're concerned about a young student who is having difficulty relating his experiences in class. During sharing time this morning, for example, he tried to tell a story about something that happened on the bus, but it didn't take long before the other students grew impatient, the teacher confused, and the student frustrated. What questions could we ask to help us get a sense of his communicative breakdown? Initially, we might ask:

- In which contexts is he able to relate his experiences more effectively? What are some of the differences between contexts in which he is successful and those in which he is not? Is he more successful sharing his experiences in smaller groups or with just one other person? Maybe he's successful with people who know him well, a close friend or his sister. If this is so it might suggest that he has difficulty adapting the form or content of his language to different audiences, in which case it would be important for us to try to increase the range of audiences with whom he interacts.

- On what basis are his stories organized? Successful storytellers do not always have to use classic or literate storytelling formulas, but listeners will have difficulty unless stories are put together using familiar, predictable patterns. If his stories don't use a familiar structure, could this apparent problem be traced to linguistic or cultural differences? Different narrative styles are characteristic of some cultures and subcultures groups (see Michaels, 1981), and what appears to be a problem may in fact be a difference. Still, even in the case of differences, teachers may wish to help students learn narrative styles (perhaps by reading various kinds of stories to the class) that enable them to communicate their experiences with different audiences. But this has to be done with sensitivity, and without devaluing students' language and culture. We'll talk more about this in Chapter 12.

- What about the student's use of word-ordering rules in this situation? How does he use syntactic rules? Does his ordering of words confuse his listeners? In the case of older students, immature syntax might focus audience attention on the form of the student's language and lead to ridicule, causing some students to be reluctant to share their experiences at all. If syntax is a problem, we'll probably want to identify at least some of the linguistic forms that are giving the student trouble and, perhaps, encourage him to participate in situations most likely to elicit the use of these forms. Again, we'd want to consider whether or not communicative breakdowns are related to dialectical differences.

- How does he use words (that is, vocabulary) to express his needs? Perhaps his choice of words confuses his listeners? Maybe he doesn't know the word or words that would express what he wants to say, in which case we'll want to ensure that he hears a rich variety of vocabulary and tries out words himself. Or maybe he uses words his audience doesn't know. Perhaps he bores his audience by using the same words over and over or taxes them by overusing indefinites (such as *thing*), in which case, the teacher may wish to encourage him to participate in situations that demand explicitness, such as giving directions. Some students might use words that offend their audiences. Effective language users not only have adequate vocabularies, but they are also able to adapt their choice of words to their listeners and to the setting. Writing and public speeches may offer ways to encourage careful word choice.
- When communication does break down, how does the student respond? Does he try to clarify what he's said, perhaps by rephrasing or adding an explanation? Or does he even notice? This is especially important. Children (and adults) must be the ultimate evaluators of their own language use, and if they don't seem to know how to evaluate the effect their language has, teachers should work with them to help them become more effective evaluators. The teacher could, for example, tape a conversation involving a student and play it back for that student. Together they could then talk about whether it makes sense and, if not, why not.
- What do his errors or miscues tell us about how this student thinks language works? Students' errors are never random; they are always based on some tentative rule or hypothesis. We recently overheard a child say, "Where is we? [*hesitates*] Where are w-w . . . ? Where are us?" These "mistakes" tell us a lot about this child's understanding of how language works. And we should feel good about students who are willing to take risks to try out their language—this is how they'll learn.

These are just some of the questions we might ask when we observe students having difficulty using language. Some teachers may ask entirely different questions, but our response to our students, how we go about teaching them, will depend on the answers to the questions we ask. The key here isn't asking *the* question or list of questions. The important thing is to ask and never stop asking. Good assessment is a matter of continually asking questions, generating hypotheses, and testing these hypotheses.

When teachers actually try to describe how students go about using language to meet their needs instead of comparing them with other students or some arbitrary standard, they are often surprised by what they find. Anne Elliot is a teacher of students who have been labeled "language disordered." For her master's thesis, Elliot used remote microphones to study her students' language on the playground. To her surprise she never found a single example of communication breakdown when her students talked among themselves or with children in regular programs on the playground (Elliot, 1991). Similarly, Jeanette Mattioli studied the language of one severely language-delayed student she called Kate. Although Mattioli initially believed that Kate was rarely able to use language successfully, what she found was that Kate was able to use language effectively (to get her needs met) more than half the time (Mattioli, 1990). As these examples illustrate, our students will continually amaze us if we believe in them and give them opportunities to show us what they know about language.

Language as a Window into Students' Learning

Classrooms that encourage students to use language to support their learning also provide teachers with regular opportunities to discover what their students are learning; that is, what students make of instruction. Notice that we're not suggesting that teachers ask whether students have learned or not. Students are always learning. We're less interested in whether students' learning matches an arbitrary adult standard (Do they know what we know?) and more interested in the personal sense that students make of schooling.

Listening to students as they work in small- or large-group discussions may enable us to find out what they are learning. But their talk will provide us with a window on their learning only if we listen carefully. Consider the following example from Joan Newton (1988, 51):

TEACHER: Henry wanted an annulment. But the Pope, the head of the church, said, "No."

PUPIL 1: Is that a divorce?

TEACHER: Not quite. Anyway, in order to bring that about, Henry had to cut away from the R.C. church of the time, and establish his own church. It was later called the Church of England, and Henry made himself the head of it so that there would be no more trouble. He divorced Catherine, and married Anne. Now that gives us an idea of why England broke with Rome, more a matter of a king's personal desires than a country's religious conviction.

PUPIL 1: Where is that church?

TEACHER: In England, although the Anglican Church is here in Canada, too. The church opposite the Safeway is an Anglican church.

PUPIL 2: But there's still a Pope.

TEACHER: I didn't say there wasn't, but the Anglican church does not see him as head of the church at all. Let's go on. Anne gave birth to a daughter who later became the first Queen Elizabeth; our queen is the second one. When the queen didn't please the king, what do you think he did?

PUPIL 3: Built another church?

TEACHER: What? No, he had her beheaded. He said she was a traitor. Do you know what a traitor is?

PUPIL 3: Someone who betrays the government. Right?

TEACHER: Right. So poor Anne also was killed. So it was all for nothing, really.

PUPIL 2: Did he get married again?

TEACHER: Indeed he did. Several times. But the Protestant church remained the most important church in England, and is so today.

Notice how much talking the teacher did relative to his students. The students didn't have much of a chance to make their own sense of the lesson, nor did the teacher allow himself the opportunity to discover what they were learning. There is good reason to believe that the students' understanding of "church" is different from that of the teacher's: for them, "church" is a building, but the teacher is talking about it as an institution. In this exchange, if students had been able to participate more and if the teacher had listened to them more carefully, he might have discovered this confusion.

Contrast this situation with the following example, also from Newton (1988, 52). This class discussion is part of a science lesson on the laws of nature following individual work.

TEACHER: Then start with the part of the problem you *do* know. What are some laws we have to obey?

ALICE: Murder. But that's not science.

TEACHER: You mean you must not murder?

ALICE: Yes. It's a law.

TEACHER: But people do, so there's some choice. Can you think of a law in which we have no choice?

BOB: We have to die. And eat.

TEACHER: Are those laws, Alice?

ALICE: No. Laws are not that. They're written up. This is stupid.

JOHN: It's a law. You have to die.

ALICE: It's not a law. Who said you have to?

JOHN: It's a natural law. Everything in nature dies.

TRACEY: Some trees don't. Stones, there's no law for stones.

WARREN: Stones aren't like nature.

GORDON: Laws apply to living things.

ALICE: No there's gravity.

TOM: Einstein made those laws.

TEACHER: Let's sort out our different meanings of law.

Here the students are active participants, and the teacher uses what he learns from their talk to shift the discussion to the different meanings of "law."

As we've said before, learning is, by definition, the integration of new knowledge with old knowledge. For students, talk is an important way to learn. For teachers, talk is a way of finding out what students are learning.

The Effects of Instruction on Students' Language

For every question about students' language there is a related question about the language-learning environment. If our students don't do something—talk, learn, solve problems, and so on—we must consider the potential of the language-learning environment, including our lessons, to encourage them to do it.

If, for example, we find that our students rarely talk in class, we should attempt to assess the effects of the environment. Do students find the materials and activities in our classrooms interesting? If students aren't talking, perhaps they don't. We should also evaluate how effective the materials and activities are in stimulating talk over the long term. When Ian was two years old he sat and watched the movie *Earth Girls Are Easy* without saying a word. The next day, however, he rambled on about the movie for hours. Similarly, an interesting classroom activity may seem to kindle little talk at the time but might inspire a flood of language on the playground, the next day, or at home. (Since teachers can't directly observe students at home they should be alert to ways of encouraging parents to share useful information about their children's language and learning.)

We will also want to consider the effect of the physical setup of the classroom on students' talk. Does the arrangement of desks and chairs encourage interaction? Perhaps we should experiment with alternative arrangements. In his reading class Dudley-Marling tried to encourage interaction during large-group discussions by asking the teachers taking the course to arrange their chairs in a horseshoe, but lively discussions were rare. One night the regular classroom was unavailable and the class moved to another room where everyone had to sit around a large table. The effect on talk was dramatic. Students shared and interacted more at that session than they had at any other time during the course.

Some teachers develop centers designed to encourage social interaction and talk but find that students never seem to visit them. If this happens, it might be helpful to experiment with the physical placement of these centers as well as their content. Students may not visit a center off in a corner of the room simply because they can't see it from their desks (see Loughlin and Martin, 1987) or because there's something more interesting between their desks and the corner (lots of people to stop to talk to).

If students don't speak out in class as much as we'd like, we might also wonder if they feel as safe about risk taking as we think they do. Perhaps, unintentionally, we evaluate students' language and respond to our intentions instead of theirs. Or maybe the supportive classroom community we thought we'd developed still hasn't matured.

When students don't learn, when they don't make school learning their own, we should ask ourselves if we're giving them enough opportunities to bring their background knowledge to our lessons. Toni's teacher began talking about

Pooh Bear before reading a story to the class, and four-year-old Toni volunteered that he had a Pooh Bear at home. The teacher said, "Oh, do you?" and then went on, missing a valuable language-learning opportunity.

Similarly, if some students are using language for relatively few purposes, we need to consider the effect of the environment. Dillon and Searle (1981) describe a classroom in which students never used language for problem solving, presumably because the teacher's lessons and activities didn't require or encourage them to use language for this purpose.

Teachers will also be interested in assessing the effectiveness of small groups. They may put students in small groups but what actually goes on? In our teaching, we've observed graduate students in groups of three or four who seemed to have difficulty getting beyond discussing their day at school. We considered the particular grouping of students, since, as we've discovered, students who know each other well don't always work well together. We also considered the nature of the group task, the product, and so on. And we realized that these students (like their younger counterparts) sometimes need to talk through their day before they get down to work.

Sometimes the best approach is to involve the students themselves in evaluation. How do they feel about the quality of group discussion? Are they learning? What are they learning? What suggestions do they have for improving effectiveness? These questions could be the basis for both small- and large-group discussions. How students feel about small-group discussion will also tell us something about their thinking on teaching and learning. Do they believe that the teacher's job is to transmit knowledge and theirs is to absorb it? If so, we'll want to confront these beliefs.

We should also look closely at our own behavior. How do we respond to students' language? What kinds of questions do we ask? Do we try to negotiate sense with our students or do we give them only our sense of things? Do we communicate an interest in what they have to say? Perhaps we don't communicate the same level of interest to all students. One of the best language teachers we know taped her interactions with her students as part of a class assignment. She discovered that in general she was a good listener when her students talked to her. But she was astonished to find that she routinely cut one student off whenever he initiated a conversation with her. If she hadn't looked closely at her own behavior, she might never have discovered that she responded to that student differently.

Teachers who examine their lessons and their behavior aren't looking for evidence of what they've done wrong, just for evidence of what they're actually doing. And sometimes we may be doing better than we think. A junior high school teacher we know was disappointed in the quality of talk as she observed six thirteen-year-old girls discussing their plans to make a rock video for a class assignment. But when we listened to a tape of this small-group discussion, we got a different impression. We heard a group of students negotiating, problem solving, and making group decisions, demonstrating sensitivity to each other's ideas and using their own knowledge base.

Ongoing assessment means constantly evaluating the interaction of our lessons, our behavior, the physical environment, and students' language in an effort to provide students with the best learning environment to meet their needs as individuals. We've asked only some of the questions that could be asked about the classroom language-learning environment. But we can only assess what goes on in our classrooms in terms of what we want to happen, that is, our goals for instruction.

Giving students frequent opportunities to talk throughout the day and across the curriculum is crucial for their language development and learning. But it isn't enough to get students to start talking. Teachers want to be sure that the quality of classroom talk supports their goals for student language and learning. Idle chatter may encourage language learning, but collaborative talk relating to the ongoing acquiring of knowledge supports both language development and learning.

Teachers assess the quality of the language and learning opportunities in their classroom by adopting the inquiring stance of researchers. By observing students talking over a period of time and in a variety of activities, they will begin to ask new questions and revise the kinds of learning experiences they provide students in their classrooms. Teachers' observations also supply information that allows them to be responsive to their legitimate need to evaluate students, communicate with parents and administrators, plan and adapt instruction, and satisfy themselves about the effects of instruction. Teachers who carefully observe their students as they engage in learning and respond to instruction learn about their students and about their own teaching. In this way, they are better able to respond to their own needs and the individual needs of their students.

11 *The Meaning of Our Lessons*

Assessing the language-learning environment in our classrooms isn't limited to examining the effects of instruction on students' language. It's just as important to consider fundamental questions about the meaning of our lessons—the pedagogical assumptions that underpin our classroom practice. These assumptions reflect our belief system and, although they are rarely articulated, we can't escape the consequences of our own theories or beliefs about teaching and learning.

Teachers make curricular choices based on their beliefs about how (or whether) knowledge is transmitted, the value of technical language, the prescriptive nature of the curriculum, the role of speculation, and the relationship of authority to the control of classroom activity (Barnes, 1976). The choices that teachers make in these areas become as much a part of the actual curriculum as the content and skills they usually view as the basic components of the curriculum. The choices we as teachers make, and the assumptions on which these choices are based, become an important focus for assessment.

To illustrate the kinds of instructional choices teachers make, how these choices relate to teachers' goals and beliefs, and, ultimately, how these choices relate to the language used by students, we present three versions of a familiar classroom activity, "sharing time."

Three Approaches to Sharing Time

The examples of sharing time we present come from three different classes of primary-aged students with learning disabilities, each containing eight to ten students. We also include excerpts from interviews we conducted with the

107

teachers of these classes about their intentions during sharing time.

SHARING TIME IN MRS. PAINTER'S CLASS

For the first example, we refer readers to the "news time" session in Mrs. Painter's class on pages 44–46. As we observed, each day after morning exercises, students gathered on the carpet while Mrs. Painter sat on a chair in front of them and invited them to share their news. Students raised their hand and, when recognized by the teacher, presented their news. For this session, David had brought a metal kidney dish as a souvenir of his stay in the hospital. Because he had something to show he requested a change in routine ("Should I get up there?") and came to the front of the class. After showing the dish, but before his sharing was finished, he returned to the group and sat down. This return is signaled by the teacher's question, "Where are you going to put that?"

After David's initial demonstration, all interaction was between the teacher and individual students. When a student asked about David's experience ("Did he have to go to sleep?"), he directed his question to Mrs. Painter. The students listened to each other, but their reactions were directed to the teacher. Mrs. Painter did not redirect these comments to the students but engaged with questioners herself.

The teacher was clearly the focus of talk during this sharing segment. We get some sense of the reasons for this arrangement by considering Mrs. Painter's expectations for sharing time and her explicit notions of language development. Speaking of her program, Mrs. Painter stressed her aim in participating in sharing time:

> We do have quite a long news time in the morning. And that's very conscious, that everybody gets a chance to say something, and sometimes it goes longer, probably, than I intended it to go, but I think it's very important that I tell my news at that time, if I can at all, but we share, so that's definitely conscious.

It's interesting that Mrs. Painter sees giving her news as part of the purpose of sharing time. She spoke further about the kind of talk she hoped would emerge.

Well I think that if we get some discussion going there's some giving and taking. I would hope that the children are hopefully going to listen to each other and are, you know, showing even interest in other people as people, not always just for the academic thing or something like that, so that's important.

The students did participate in sharing time and did listen attentively. But the "give-and-take" aspect of the discussion —one of Mrs. Painter's stated goals—was missing.

Mrs. Painter also indicated her interest in the emotional and personal values that emerged from sharing-time discussions: "You often pick up moods, like Ron is a moody little boy and, if he's sitting there glumly or something, I can maybe talk to him quietly and maybe avoid other problems."

Mrs. Painter took the view, in a general sense, that there needed to be an authentic basis for language use before it would contribute to students' overall language development. Speaking of teaching specific aspects of language development, she said:

> And given a little bit of isolated language they may be able to perform something that they're not going to do automatically when they're involved in other . . . but these kinds of things are certainly things that are suggested we use. And I do a little bit of it, but I'm never convinced that this is the way, and I think that language has to exist in a little different, in its natural state.

Applying this specifically to news time, she said: "If I'm prying and pulling and prodding, then probably that's not a good morning for news. I mean, you don't always have something exciting happening every night, do you?"

Implicit in Mrs. Painter's practice is an unstated goal: to engage students in slightly more formal or adultlike conversations. At times, for example, she elevated her own vocabulary, hoping to stretch the children's language. This approach is demonstrated in two comments relating to blood sampling. She replies, "Isn't that *provoking* when that happens?" and "They couldn't get a sample of my blood no matter what they did so they said, 'We'll get a *pediatric needle*' and, *that's a child's* 'cause it was smaller, so I know what that's like."

How does Mrs. Painter's organization of this language event embed her beliefs and help her achieve her goals? One of her explicit goals is to develop bonds between herself and her students and between students. Toward this end, she has created a climate in which children have the conversational "space" that allows them to talk. When she enters into a one-to-one dialogue with a child, she provides an attentive audience and conversational partner. Her participation also prevents undue interruption and requires that the other students wait their turn. The lack of prodding allows children to tell their news in their own way. Although Mrs. Painter indicates that developing relationships among the students is a goal, it is more difficult to see how these relationships are fostered. The give-and-take is usually absent and is, in fact, inhibited by the practice of channeling all communication through the teacher. Through her own interest, however, she does give students the confidence to speak. And students learn about each other and appear interested enough to listen. Mrs. Painter encourages participation— another explicit goal—through questioning and sharing personal experiences, which stimulates further response. By controlling participation, she is able to draw students into the discussion and prevent domination by a few speakers. And all students are given a chance to share and respond.

Mrs. Painter indicated her skepticism about teaching bits of "isolated language" and her belief that language "has to exist in its natural state." She used news time as a vehicle for promoting talk because she believed that this would give talk a basis in experience. She didn't expect children to make up news, nor was there a demand for participation. Her own responses focused on the ideas expressed, and she encouraged children to use each other's topics as a basis for sharing their own experiences.

In general, Mrs. Painter's control of the situation, maintained by channeling all talk through her, serves to formalize, elevate, and give value to the talk. Her personal, authentic response develops the emotional rapport that invites and encourages talk.

SHARING TIME IN MRS. CLAY'S CLASS

We observed a different version of sharing time in Mrs. Clay's class. Here, presenters stood in front of the class beside the teacher. After they had shown their personal treasures, other students raised their hands and the speaker invited their questions. The teacher intervened at any time.

In this excerpt it was Larry's turn to share. He brought a Transformer toy and stood in front of the class to show it.

TEACHER: Larry, do you have something to share?
LARRY: Yes, Mrs. Clay . . . [*Pause*] Keith?
KEITH: What is it?
LARRY: It's a Transformer.
SANDRA: Can you show us how to transform it?
LARRY: It's easy. [*He demonstrates.*] Keith?
KEITH: What is its name?
LARRY: Beachcomber. Keith?
KEITH: Who gave it to you?
LARRY: My friend, for my birthday, last . . .
KEITH: Is he a bad guy or a good guy?
LARRY: Good guy. Keith?
KEITH: When was your birthday?
LARRY: October the sixth. Keith?
KEITH: Do you . . .
TEACHER: Is Keith the only one who wants to ask questions today?
LARRY: Pardon?
KEITH: [*Inaudible*]
TEACHER: You guys are always bringing Transformers. What does that word mean . . . transformer?
KEITH: To transform.
TEACHER: Well, what does that mean?
LARRY: They could change into stuff.
TEACHER: Yeah. Transform means change. That's good.
JOHN: There is a transformer on the TV. It's a transformer.
KEITH: Like . . .
TEACHER: What did you say John?
JOHN: A transformer and a TV. There's . . .
TEACHER: Is that the same kind of thing?
JOHN: No.
TEACHER: Oh, what's it do?
JOHN: It . . . ah, my dad told me it's called a transformer.
TEACHER: Part of the workings of the television . . . is that what you're thinking?
JOHN: Um hmm.
TEACHER: Yes, you're right. Yes, Keith?
KEITH: Can you play with it much?
LARRY: Um hmm.

TEACHER: Did you tell us, does he have a name?

LARRY: Yeah, Beachcomber.

TEACHER: Oh, I'm sorry, I'd forgotten that.

LARRY: Keith?

KEITH: Do you . . . which Autobot do you like best?

LARRY: I like all of them.

TEACHER: What did you just call that, Keith? I missed what you said.

KEITH: Autobot. The good guys are called the Autobots and the bad guys are called the Deceptacons.

TEACHER: Ah . . . they're called what?

KEITH: Autobots.

TEACHER: Autobots. Okay. What's the other one? What are the bad guys?

KEITH: Deceptacons.

TEACHER: Deceptacons. What's that mean?

KEITH: I don't know. Bad.

TEACHER: Oh.

MORLEY: Deceptacons. Autobots.

KEITH: Almost all of them are planes and jets.

TEACHER: Okay. That's a big word. Deceptacons . . . do you know how to spell those words?

LARRY: I do. I have it in my book.

KEITH: I know.

TEACHER: When you write your journals for me this morning, let's see if you can use those words. I don't know how to spell them.

LARRY: I know how to spell . . .

TEACHER: I might be able to spell Autobot, but I don't know how to spell Deceptacon.

LARRY: A-u-t-o-b-o-t-s.

TEACHER: Okay, I think I could manage that one but I don't know about Deceptacon.

In this version of sharing time, most of the comments were brief and straightforward. But there is considerable student-student interaction as students direct a series of inquiries to the presenter, augmented by questions and proddings from the teacher. Five of the eight students speak at least once in this brief excerpt.

An interesting feature, which isn't communicated in the transcript, is that Larry directed most of his talk to the teacher. He called on students to ask questions but directed his answers to Mrs. Clay. She, in turn, spoke specifically to Larry and directed general statements to the class. The students in the group addressed their questions to Larry and answered Mrs. Clay's questions.

Mrs. Clay intervened in the discussion for a variety of reasons. She extended the process: "Is Keith the only one who wants to ask questions today?" She tried to develop vocabulary: "What does that word mean . . . Transformer?" She questioned to extend her own knowledge: "What are the bad guys?" She related the session to the journal-writing task: "Do you know how to spell those words?"

Mrs. Clay's goals for sharing time were different from Mrs. Painter's. Mrs. Clay focused on developing certain aspects of language and interaction and used sharing time explicitly as a vehicle for language development. She outlined her intentions and her approach thus:

> Sharing time in the morning used to revolve around nothing but "I got a toy, this was for my birthday" or you know, something that came from my home that they reported on at first, and there really wasn't a lot of interaction, or if there was, if someone had a question, they would ask the same question over and over again. So what we started off doing, I would bring something like, I brought a potato peeler one day [*inaudible*]. I held it up and just said, "Now I'm not going to tell you a thing about what I have in my hand. You have to . . . you ask me questions." Now, for these children to ask questions . . . [it] took me a long, long time to get them to be able to use the "when's" and the "where's" and the "why's." And I used to have them look up on the board [where she had written Where? When? Why? What?]. I would, you know, you would see them looking. Thinking of a word that would help them begin a question. And it was a skill that I thought they were really weak in, and I wanted to develop the ability to be able to ask reasonable questions that would help them learn. So that's why I do that type of thing in the morning.

Mrs. Clay's explicit purpose for sharing time was to get students to ask appropriate, well-constructed questions. Her organization of sharing time related well to this goal. Students shared their treasures primarily by responding to questions as their classmates drew upon a small body of questions they were prepared to ask. There was little extended interaction, but that wasn't the goal of the activity.

An unstated goal of Mrs. Clay's sharing time is to encourage students to use the topic of sharing time for their journal-writing activity, which followed. Mrs. Clay often wrote down words or sentences from sharing time and invited students to use these "notes" for writing in their journals.

This excerpt, like the earlier one from Mrs. Painter's sharing time, illustrates once again how a particular view of language development leads to particular aims and strategies. Mrs. Clay sees language as a set of rules and forms to be learned and used through practice. The content of sharing time becomes a vehicle for practicing these forms. As students practice, their statements are short, simple, and predictable. Answers are less important than questions—Mrs. Clay's aim is not to use response to develop ideas, but to use response to build vocabulary. Notably, the one time that Mrs. Clay focuses on content—by requesting more information about names and characterization—it leads to the most developed, sustained language in the segment.

SHARING TIME IN MRS. HANLON'S CLASS

The final example of sharing time we present comes from Mrs. Hanlon's class. In this class, students wrote in their personal diaries first and then used these diaries as the basis for their news time. Writing in their diaries first was intended to ensure that students would have something personal to talk about.

Like the other two classes, students gathered in a circle for sharing time, but, unlike the other two teachers, Mrs. Hanlon did not sit in front of the class. Instead, she picked a student to lead news time while she sat behind her students. The student "leader" called on two or three students to share their news. As students shared they led a conversation about their news. Here is a typical news time session in Mrs. Hanlon's class.

MARK: [*Reading from his journal*] "Tuesday, May 27, 19—." This is the other part of it. "Yesterday [*inaudible*]." Can I read all of it?

TEACHER: Certainly.

MARK: "Monday, May 26, 19—. On the weekend I went to Canada's Wonderland [*a large amusement park*]."

TERRY: What did you see there?

MARK: "Tuesday, May 27, 19—. I saw lots of rides and lots of people in the water."

TERRY: Did you see any games?

ALLEN: You should have wrote that.

MARK: [*Inaudible*]

ALLEN: Did you go on the new fun ride?

ROGER: I went on that thing and it was so boring.

TEACHER: What do you do?

ROGER: You just go in a little circle and you go down this little, you know, it just goes down like that and you're sort of a [*inaudible*]. It's no fun, you just go around in a circle twice.

MARK: [*Inaudible*]

ROGER: Well maybe . . . boring . . .

TERRY: Did you go on the monster, go on the beast?

MARK: [*Inaudible*]

ROGER: Oh, that's not scary.

MARK: You look straight down, you're going down and it's straight in the front car. It really is scary. Ken?

KEN: Did you go this Saturday?

MARK: Last Saturday. Yeah, last Saturday.

KEN: Did you see any firecrackers?

MARK: No, it wasn't that good . . . I can't go back again until [*inaudible*].

TERRY: . . . the color . . .

TEACHER: Allison has a question. Then we'll move on to the next person.

Mark began by reading a brief entry from his journal. The other students then asked him questions about his visit to Canada's Wonderland, a place with which most of them were familiar, and soon began sharing their own experiences and opinions. There was considerable interaction among the students. The teacher intervened only twice—once to ask a question and once to exert control. Although the teacher had little role in conducting the discussion, the students remained focused on the topic.

In her interview, Mrs. Hanlon reveals a consistency between the pattern of interaction during news time and her goals and beliefs about language:

I would think that they would just tend to do that [*interact with each other*] if you don't interrupt them too much.

Like, I really don't interrupt them, tend to lead it all the time . . . I would just, by not saying anything then they tend to talk. I never assume the leadership role during that time. Initially, at the beginning of the year, I didn't have them playing teacher the way they like to do now, but I still tried to stay out of it. I found that it was easier with someone else in charge, and it was so interesting to see the kind of mimicking they would do. "I'm not going to start until everyone's sitting nicely" kind of mimicking the students often do. *I found that the less I talked, the more they talked.*

It is important to Mrs. Hanlon that her students have opportunities to use talk to work through their own difficulties. She sees, even in their mimicking, that they have the resources to use their language but need situations that encourage them to talk. Her statement that "the less I talked the more they talked" is a sign of recognition that, as teacher-leader, she could easily interfere with the use of language she is trying to encourage. So she moved herself out of the center of the interaction. Mrs. Hanlon also believes that students need "a chance . . . to communicate with each other, to get feedback from their peers," but she wishes the communication to occur in "more and more real life situations than having to be formal all the time. They don't get a chance to do that." This informality is reflected in the interaction among students.

The Relationship Between Our Theories and Our Practice

The differences in these three approaches to sharing time illustrate how teachers' language goals—which are informed by their conscious and unconscious beliefs about language and language learning—influence their teaching practices. Mrs. Painter used sharing time to build relationships between herself and her students, so she placed herself in the center of the discussion. Mrs. Hanlon wanted news time to provide students with an opportunity to talk informally together, so she distanced herself from the group and signaled her withdrawal by naming a student as discussion leader. She also regarded sharing time as a language-development activity;

since she believed that language is developed by meaningful use, her role was to provide opportunities for students to use language. Conversely, Mrs. Painter didn't see sharing time in the context of language development. For her, it had more to do with learning to get along and building self-esteem. She made sure that students had a chance to be heard and used her response to encourage students to talk about their experiences.

Mrs. Clay approached sharing time from a different perspective. Like Mrs. Hanlon, she saw it as a language-development activity, but from her perspective, in contrast to Mrs. Hanlon's, language is developed by learning and practicing specific language forms. She encouraged a more ritualistic format, in which students practiced set approaches to questioning.

It is important for us as teachers to realize that although our goals influence our classroom decisions, there are instances when our classroom decisions may unknowingly prevent us from achieving our goals. If teachers don't think about language when planning activities they may, in fact, miss opportunities to enhance their own teaching or unfortunately may make decisions that conflict with their language goals. Mrs. Hanlon, for example, always had student-to-student talk as a goal, but her initial decision to lead discussions herself actually stopped students from talking to each other. Realizing this she removed herself from the leadership role and more student-to-student talk resulted.

Similarly, it would frustrate students if we encouraged them to hypothesize and speculate in discussion and then announced that we were going to grade them on their efforts. There is an old joke about a school in which students were encouraged to talk and write about their personal interests. A student warned a new classmate, "Your turtle is neat, but don't show it to the teacher or you'll have to write something about it." We need to be alert to these subtle conflicts, which can easily sabotage our language goals.

The decisions we make in our classrooms are never arbitrary—they are based on our fundamental beliefs about teaching and learning and the nature of what it is we're teaching. But we don't always articulate our beliefs, nor are our practices always consistent with them. We may say that we care about what students have to say, for example, but our classroom practices may indicate otherwise.

Ultimately, the beliefs we demonstrate in practice are more important than the beliefs we claim to espouse. The challenge for us is to examine our teaching carefully to get a sense of what those implicit beliefs are and how they affect learning in our classrooms.

12 Teaching Language to Linguistically Different Students

Teachers are increasingly likely to work in schools in which more than one variety of English is spoken. Because of increased immigration many teachers may also work with students who speak relatively little English or with ESL students, for whom English is a second language. In general, we believe that everything in this book applies to the language learning of all students, including those from different linguistic backgrounds. But to be effective with linguistically different students, teachers also need to understand the meaning of linguistic differences and the effect these differences will have on their efforts to encourage language development. In this chapter we discuss some of the issues associated with linguistic differences that are most important to language educators.

The Meaning of Language Differences

As we have said, language is a tool for getting things done, a means by which its users fulfill their needs. But speakers of different languages don't get things done in the same ways. Besides the obvious lexical, phonological, and grammatical variations between one language and another, there are also cultural differences, which determine what people talk about (students from some cultures may not be willing to discuss feelings with strangers, including their teachers), who they talk to (in some cultures children may, out of respect for their elders, rarely initiate talk with adults), and how they talk to them (students from some cultures may, again out of respect for adults, refuse to look their teachers "in the eye").

In addition to these cultural differences in the ways language is used there are also *arbitrary and relatively slight* (see Labov, 1972) dialectical variations in the phonological, grammatical, and lexical systems within languages them-selves. But like linguistic variation across languages, dialecti-cal differences are just that—differences. Preferred dialects (the variety of English spoken on the evening news, for example) are preferred because they are spoken by the majority, by the rich and powerful, or both. Even though a preferred dialect can make no claim to inherent superiority over other varieties of English, its speakers may have better access to certain jobs or social groups for reasons which should be obvious.

All ways of speaking may be equal in terms of their lin-guistic, if not their social potential, but different ways of speaking do not have the same meanings for their speakers. Language and culture are inextricably related. How we talk, the meanings we choose to make and how we choose to make them, is determined, in part, by how we relate to the world and the people in it. Our cultural backgrounds—the kinship patterns, the rituals and beliefs, the childrearing prac-tices, and so on that we share with members of our group—influence what we mean and how we mean. The way people talk is thus an important part of their personal and cultural identity. Change that and we change who they are and how they see the world.

Social and cultural identity also help explain the mainte-nance of intra-language differences and the ability of accents and dialects to resist the homogenizing effects of the mass media. In the words of Frank Smith, we use language to claim "membership" in clubs. The Dudley-Marling children once had a babysitter from Jamaica who, although she spoke with an accent, was easy to understand. When she spoke to her Jamaican friends, however, she would switch to her West Indian dialect, which we were not able to understand. She used her West Indian dialect as a means of saying that al-though she lives in Canada, being Jamaican is still an impor-tant part of who she is. Similarly, teenagers talk the way they do as a means of signaling belonging to one group—teens—and not to another group—adults. And dockworkers talk "like dockworkers" or computer programmers "like com-puter programmers" because that is who they are.

We can just as easily use language to say "I'm not one of you" or "I'm no longer one of you" as we can to say "I'm one of you." Searle, for example, tells a story about his expe-rience visiting secondary schools in England. He found that students whose families had emigrated from the West Indies sometimes exaggerated their dialects when they spoke with each other in front of their teachers. This effectively excluded teachers and probably caused some resentment. The students' actions were clearly a deliberate attempt to say, "You're not one of us." When their teachers employed a very formal English they may have unconsciously, but just as effectively signaled, "I'm not one of you either."

The relationship between language and group membership may be a source of conflict for some people trying to get ahead in the world, since getting ahead can mean changing the way you talk. Families of nonmainstream speakers, for example, may be proud of their children's academic achievements, reflected in part by their new ways of talking, but at the same time worry that their children's adoption of the "dialect of power" may indicate rejection of their families and their culture. In Western cultures we tend to believe that everyone wants to better themselves socially and economically, and perhaps they do. But some people may have to pay a high price for social mobility. Others may reject "upward" mobility altogether, concluding that the costs are too high.

How we talk says a lot about who we are and where we've come from, but the ways of speaking we share with others in our social, ethnic, socioeconomic, cultural, or vocational groups say nothing about the quality of our thinking. The overwhelming majority of language educators support the conclusion that "all natural languages are equally capable of conveying ideas of great complexity" (Marland, 1977, 48). To believe otherwise risks seeing children's language and their thinking through the lens of stereotype and prejudice. Referring to the variety of English spoken by some urban black children, for example, William Labov (1972) warns educators:

When the everyday language of black children is seen as "not a language at all" and "not possessing the means for logical thought," the effect of such labeling is repeated many times each day during the school year. . . . When teachers hear him say *I don't want none* or *They mine,* they will be hearing . . . not an English dialect different from theirs, but the "primitive mentality of the savage mind." (230–231)

In some cases linguistic and cultural differences may lead to misunderstandings between students and teachers. We once saw a videotape of a lesson that took place in a school for Native American children in the southwestern United States. At one point in the lesson the teacher asked a young boy a question he was unable to answer. The teacher then asked the same question of several other students, who responded by bowing their heads and saying nothing. Apparently, the teacher concluded, no one knew the answer to her question. The students' use of language, however, in this case their nonuse of language, indicated more about a set of social relations, "You don't shame your brother or sister," than about their knowledge of the subject matter. Similarly, Maija Searle recalls her first-grade teacher's impatience with her slow and deliberate approach to her work, which led the teacher to keep Maija in at recess to complete her work. Her teacher was unaware that Maija's Finnish parents had admonished her to "do everything carefully and well." In another example of culturally induced misunderstanding, we've been told that some Native American children do not have a word for "please" in their native language and don't use the word *please* in English either. This leads some of their teachers to conclude unfairly that these children are rude. Similarly, Ward (1971) observed that some children are puzzled when teachers ask a question to which they already know the answer, since in their experience, it is assumed that if someone asks a question it is because they don't know the answer. And Heath (1985) reported that some of the children she observed had difficulty interpreting teachers' hints and indirect requests ("It's time to tidy up now"), leading teachers to conclude that either the students didn't understand or they were being deliberately uncooperative. Heath notes that in these children's experience, if adults wanted something done they told them so directly ("Clean up your room").

So some students may have occasional difficulties in school because of disparities between the language and expectations of their teachers and their own language and cultural experiences. But in general, students' dialects should not affect their ability to participate in the academic and social life of schooling. In our opinion, the degree to which dialectical and cultural differences do lead to difficulties has more to do with our sensitivity to linguistic and cultural differences and our ability to accommodate differences than to any limitations in students' language.

Respecting Language Differences

Effective language users adjust both the form and content of their language according to demands imposed on them by the physical setting, the audience, and so on. Most of us would use much more formal language in speaking to the superintendent of schools in her office than to a close friend at a party.

Similarly, in some circumstances, typically those in which formal English is usually most appropriate, speakers may be more successful using a standard English dialect than some other variety of English. Speakers of dialects other than standard English, for reasons that are arbitrary but real, may be disadvantaged in certain social and vocational situations.

From our perspective as teachers, however, the emphasis must be on increasing students' dialectical range, helping students learn the features of standard English as another dialect, *not as a replacement* for their dialects, which can mean sacrificing their cultural and linguistic identity. Fluency in standard English may seem to be a student's ticket to vocational and social mobility, but speakers of nonmainstream dialects can reasonably aspire to a variety of useful, high-paying careers even without adopting standard English. In fact, the formal English of their teachers may even interfere with their ability to get along in some of these jobs.

Ideally, the ability to manipulate a range of dialectical features will be only a part of students' ongoing efforts to adjust the form and content of their language to the demands of the social context, but the choice must be theirs. They must see the need. We can't give students our ways of speaking or make them speak the way we do, not without risking a terrible cost to their personal and cultural identities.

Teachers' respect for students' linguistic and cultural identities will be an important factor in the degree to which they are able to affect students' willingness to use features of standard English as an appropriate conversational strategy. Teachers who consciously or unconsciously signal a lack of respect for students' language only encourage students to reject mainstream culture and the varieties of English associated with it, using their dialects as a means of symbolizing their exclusion and establishing solidarity even though it may trap them on the lowest rungs of the economic ladder (Apple, 1985).

Part of respecting cultural and linguistic differences is being aware that certain ways of talking, and therefore, certain ways of teaching language, may conflict with the cultural values of some students and their parents. Guided by studies of the language of parents to their children, for example, some language authorities advise teachers and parents, especially teachers and parents of language-delayed children, to use language-teaching strategies such as encouraging children to initiate language, following their conversational leads, expanding their elliptical utterances, and so on. Although there is the potential danger that the deliberate use of these strategies can unintentionally distract parents' and teachers' from their natural communicative intent, these are basically sensible approaches. We've recommended similar strategies in previous chapters. But these strategies are derived primarily from studies of the language of middle-class North American parents to their children and are not universal. In some cultures, parents do not expand their children's utterances and children are not encouraged to initiate talk. In other cultures, children are not seen by adults to be worthy conversational partners and little is said to them (Blount, 1977; Heath, 1985; Ward, 1971). The ways parents have of talking with their children have as much to do with culture and the relationship of parents and their children in that culture as they do with the teaching and learning of language. The point here is this: As teachers we need to be sensitive to cultural differences and the fact that encouraging certain ways of talking in children whose cultures are different from ours may create serious cultural conflicts, especially for parents who are anxious for their children to succeed in school but are also eager for their children to retain their cultural identity. We aren't suggesting that language teachers do nothing when working with culturally and linguistically different students, only that they be circumspect about the possibility that the effects of the language-learning environment they create in their classrooms can sometimes be negative.

Respect for and understanding of linguistic and cultural differences may also affect teachers' assessment of students' language. Verbal behaviors they may have seen as deviant, delayed, or illogical will be recognized as merely different. In general, we as teachers will be much more cautious about evaluating the language of students from culturally and linguistically different backgrounds, acknowledging that whenever we hear students talk we are also observing their culture. One of the most striking examples of the influence of the sociocultural context on children's use of language, and the assessment of their language, comes from Labov's (1972) study of black youths in Harlem. Some researchers in the mid-1960s described the monosyllabic utterances of some black children and concluded that these children had virtually no language at all (see Bereiter et al., 1966). Labov himself describes similar examples of "limited language" in black youths interviewed by both white and black adults. But when one of these boys (Leon) was interviewed a second time by the same black adult (Clarence) in another social context, a different picture emerged. In this instance Clarence brought along Leon's best friend and a supply of potato chips, sat down on the floor with Leon, and introduced taboo words and topics. Now Leon had quite a lot to say and actively competed for the chance to speak. This study is a powerful reminder of the effect of social context on children's language behavior: what you see is not necessarily what you get. In a comment important to anyone interested in assessment, Labov concludes that "the social situation is the most powerful determinant of verbal behavior and . . . an adult must enter into the right social relation with a child if he wants to find out what a child can do" (212). In general, teachers working with culturally and linguistically different students need to ask a lot of questions and should never be too confident they've found the answers.

The Role of Teachers

The principles of language learning we discussed in Chapter 2 apply to everyone learning language, including students learning English as a second language. The focus must still be on communication—creating opportunities for students to use English and hear English used to fulfill their own authentic communicative intentions in a range of contexts. Students must be at the center of their own language learning in settings in which they are free to try out and experiment with language, without fear of correction or evaluation.

Drills, workbooks, and other exercises that trivialize and fragment language, and remove language learning from natural communicative contexts, have no more place in the language education of ESL students than they do in that of any other student. And the ultimate test of language learning is whether ESL students, like other language learners, are able to use language to fulfill their personal needs. Isolating students in ESL classes for most or all of the day will only reduce their opportunities to use and experience English. Everything we've discussed in previous chapters applies equally well to the education of students whose first language is English and students whose primary language is other than English.

The role of the teacher in the language education of students who use a dialect other than standard English is more complicated and delicate. Teachers care deeply for their students, and most believe that it will help students get along better in society if they are able to use standard English forms. But, as we noted earlier, people can get along in school and after school without adopting mainstream dialects. The degree to which teachers are able to influence students' willingness to try out mainstream dialects will be a function of both the respect they communicate for students' language and their own ability to create opportunities for students to discover a personal need to increase the range of dialect features they use. Direct teaching of standard dialects is no more likely to be successful than explicit teaching of any aspect of language. In any case, it's probably unnecessary since, except in the case of some immigrant children, it's hard to imagine students who haven't had an abundance of opportunities to hear standard English. And differences between dialects are few (see Labov, 1972). Direct teaching of standard English, with the implication that it's a better way of speaking, is disrespectful and potentially insulting and may only further alienate some students. Requiring standard English guarantees their alienation. Neutral activities like role playing, which give *all* students an opportunity to try out a range of dialectical features, may be useful. But again, students will not increase the range of dialectical features they use unless they find personal reasons for doing so. Teachers can't give them reasons.

Ultimately, the education of children who do not use a mainstream dialect poses a moral and ethical dilemma for teachers. Caring teachers rightfully aim to prepare students to participate in modern society. And we must acknowledge the fact that in some settings the use of standard English is preferred. But a society that judges people on the way they speak is an unjust society.

Prejudice against ways of talking associated with the lower classes, some blacks, Appalachian whites, Hispanics, or Native Americans masks even more repugnant prejudices against people based on race, culture, or ethnic origin (see Lindfors, 1980). Even as we work with the best of intentions to help our students get long in the real world, schools that stress the learning of standard English, or worse, the un-learning of nonstandard forms, may unwittingly contribute to the perpetuation of racial and ethnic prejudices and social injustice. However schools resolve this dilemma, there is clearly an important role for the schools to play here. Education can be an important tool in changing people's attitudes and in addressing the roots of social, ethnic, and racial prejudice.

There are undeniable differences within languages and between one language and another, but distinctive ways of talking among different groups of people bear no relationship to the quality of their thinking, their needs, or their worthiness as human beings. That doesn't mean that these differences are unimportant. How people talk and what they talk about are crucial to their sense of belonging and their personal identity. If we don't respect a person's language we don't respect the person either; if we don't respect our students, it's unlikely we'll have much effect on their lives.

13 "But My Children Aren't Like That!"

How do students who have language problems fit into the view of language teaching and learning we've been presenting? We view language learning in terms of the range of purposes for which children learn to use language and the settings in which they can successfully achieve those purposes. All children know something about language and can use their knowledge to some degree. Students with language problems may use language to fulfill fewer communicative intentions in fewer contexts than other children their age, but that doesn't mean they don't know or cannot use language.

Language problems are rarely absolute. They have to be understood in reference to the context in which they occur. Cazden (1988) and Tough (1976) both report that children who come from presumably impoverished language backgrounds, children especially at risk for having language problems in school, do not differ from children who have richer language backgrounds in terms of the purposes for which they use language or the language structures they use. They differ only in terms of the range of contexts in which they use these forms and structures. To understand these differences we must understand how children conceive of the context of their language use.

We must also be ready to acknowledge that all children have skills as language learners, including those who appear to be struggling to learn language. In the following excerpt (Elliott, 1991, 52–53) we see Mandie, a seven-year-old girl in a class for severely linguistically delayed children, go through a wide repertoire of language strategies to achieve her goal. Some features of Mandie's language may vary from those of other children her age, but we could never classify her as unable to use language and must appreciate the

sophistication of her knowledge. Mandie was trying to negotiate with other students for a Lego person

MANDIE: Hey you!

GERRY: What?

MANDIE: Can I have a person?

GERRY: [*No response*]

MANDIE: Can I use one like this? [*Holds up another Lego person*]

GERRY: No!

MANDIE: I don't got a person! [*Asks someone else*] Can I use
   one of your persons? [*Pleadingly*] Please!

GERRY: No!

MANDIE: Fine then, you can't go to my house [*playhouse*]
   anymore! Or you!

GERRY: Okay then, I'm not going to your birthday! [*on the
   next weekend*]

MANDIE: That's mean! Give me this person!

GERRY: [*Very definitely*] Nope!

MANDIE: [*Turns away angrily and then very nicely tries
   someone else*] Can I use your person?

PAUL: Okay!

Elliot conducted her study with children she taught. Her initial concern with relying on a remote microphone to record
speech was that the children, including Mandie, were so
severely limited, it might not be possible to collect any recog-
nizable language relying only on sound. Instead we see in
Mandie not only a clear but a very flexible communicator.
She tries demands, threats, reason, and finally a polite request
to achieve her goal.

All children are very good at learning although they may
not be equally good at it. Few of us will ever work with children who don't have any language or who don't know much
about the world they live in. All children except the very
youngest are able to fulfill communicative intentions in some
contexts, if just through the use of gestures or crying. Our
challenge isn't to give students language but to build on the
language and experiences they already have. It's when we
lose faith in what they know and in their ability to learn that
we most often resort to contriving settings for language
teaching. When this happens we forget the most important
principle of language learning: Language isn't for learning,
language is for doing things with.

The principles of language learning that have guided our discussion apply to all children regardless of their age, experience, or language ability. No one can learn how language operates in natural conversational settings without having had considerable experience with language in those settings. In fact, a good case can be made that traditional approaches to working with language problems, which emphasize fragmented bits of language, may exacerbate the difficulties of students with these problems (see, for example, Bartoli and Botel, 1988; Dudley-Marling, 1990). We have not suggested that there are no situations in which teachers may focus on particular aspects of language development; what we have advocated is that these focused incidents must be presented within an overall context of purpose and meaning (see Chapter 6). When children experience language difficulties we must continue to give them every opportunity to extend their control of language, but the basic principles of language learning do not change.

The following example from one of Mrs. Hanlon's news times demonstrates that students can gain proficiency in language when allowed to use it to develop personal meaning. We have seen how Mrs. Hanlon conducted these sessions, removing herself and sitting at the back of the group. The student, Amy, was diagnosed as "having virtually no language." School consultants recommended sending her to a special language-development class, whose curriculum would consist primarily of a series of language drills aimed at "putting language into Amy." Mrs. Hanlon felt that this would not be the answer to Amy's needs and arranged for Amy to stay in her class on the condition that she would focus on developing Amy's language. To do this, Mrs. Hanlon engaged Amy in the ongoing activities and discussions of the classroom, making sure that she didn't get "lost in the crowd." Having observed Amy in the classroom we can attest to the fact that she spent a great deal of the time without speaking, and in many interactions she was very limited in her language use. But here we see how Amy, given an audience and an engaged topic, uses and extends her language. At times, the language is not perfectly clear, and sometimes the meaning is implicit at best. It is clear that the class, by focusing on her meaning, provides the cues that allow her to develop and extend her meaning through language.

TEACHER: If there are no other questions for Mitch we'll have one more person this morning and that's it. One more.

TODD: [*Pause*] Oh, I have a question.

TEACHER: We'll have to save it now. There's just the next person.

AMY: This morning my cat, he was up and I was the only person asleep still, 'cause my mom was going to let me sleep in so the cat was, anyway he came upstairs, right [*teacher coughs*], he came back up; and he started to play with my hair and he meowed and everything and I finally woke up and then the purple things that I got out to take to school, well [*teacher coughs and turns off the mike for a moment, disrupting the sense of the tape*], and he was running all around the house and the cat was chasing after it and I was doing it from upstairs way down to the bottom and the cat was trying to get it and I let it go I think. I let it go so, so the cat came running after it and caught it right in the mouth and he was dragging it upstairs. Any questions or comments?

TODD: Was it still sticky?

AMY: Yeah it was sticky. Sticking onto the rail. Kenny?

TODD: Was he dragging it up because it was too heavy for him?

AMY: Yup. [*Laughter*] And then after a while I put it, when he didn't want to taste it so I put a blanket over my bed so the cat could sit there but he, he just, so he sat there on the blanket and he was meowing and scratching and I think 'cause he loves to go outside, 'cause there's one young and dark cat outside and we didn't know they were outside and he kept calling him up and finally, finally we heard them at the front door. [*Laughter*] John?

JOHN: Mike gave me one of the kittens his cat had.

TEACHER: [*Unintelligible*]

JOHN: No, the cat had babies. One of the kittens. And the cat had babies. She's tooken it to the vet.

TEACHER: That's interesting.

AMY: Our vet. When we didn't have a cat, our vet, Scooter's vet, was about to buy our cat and my dad's best friend has Scamp, that's Scooter's brother ...

TODD: Who's Scooter?

AMY: ... our vet was about to ... hmm? Our cat, and Scamp is Scooter's brother. Our vet was about to buy Scooter but we came earlier than him, but he's glad because, he's glad because, he, he just, he's glad because he's Scooter's vet 'cause he was going to buy Scooter so Scooter comes to visit and he's happy.

PAUL: Scooter, I got a scooter.

TODD: Ride on top of him?

TERRY: Does he just scoot around.

AMY: He scoots around.

TERRY: Does he turn into a scooter?

AMY: When we first got him he liked his bottle.

PAUL: He smashed into the wall.

AMY: Well we named him Scooter 'cause the first time I saw him, they got him two days ago, but then, the two days after I got to see him, the day I named him Scooter, so he was scooting all over the house and he was that small so he was scooting all over the house because of his teeth. He's got a place behind the stereo . . .

TODD: Behind the stereo.

AMY: And behind the TV . . . in the basement . . . and the worst job is what I have to do . . . the litter box . . .

PAUL: So do I.

TEACHER: Well there's always responsibility with having a pet.

STUDENT: I have to pick up the dog's litter in the back yard.

AMY: Mitch?

MITCH: Did you ever have to [*unintelligible*] a wire?

AMY: A what?

MITCH: For the TV or stereo?

AMY: No, but we were all watching something really important, and he was playing with the wires trying to get our attention and he pulled it out. [*Laughter*] So we had a spray bottle so when he's bad we spray him with the water. Like when he's outside and he's off the porch we usually spray him and when he's bad we usually spray him a little bit. And he was down then, so I sprayed him and so he ran right up and the door was open and my father was carrying something very fragile out the door and he raced through and almost tripped my dad. [*Laughter*]

TEACHER: Paul?

PAUL: My dad, I have to, sometimes I have to clean up the dog dirt from off the hill . . .

TEACHER: As I say, that's the responsibility that goes with being a pet owner isn't it?

It is possible to see Amy's confidence and pleasure grow as the audience laughs and questions. Certainly she displays considerable linguistic resources. The needs of the audience become the language curriculum. They clarify: "Who's Scooter?" They add: "I have to pick up the dog's litter." They extend her range of topics: "Do you ever have to [*unintelligible*] a wire?" Each of these genuine interventions contributes to Amy's understanding of language and discourse. It needs to be reemphasized that Amy has been described as, and at times behaves as if she were, severely language-restricted, yet in this context her language flourishes. Her language flows as she talks with knowledge to an interested audience. We know that an interesting topic and a sympathetic audience do not, in themselves, guarantee a successful interaction. They would seem to be a necessary condition, however, for stimulating extended language use.

When teachers say "My children aren't like that," they are substantially correct. After all, no two children are alike. All children use language in different ways at different times. Different children have different levels of success in various contexts. Despite general patterns of development there is no absolute order. What we learn depends on a wide variety of factors, including how we encounter language, what our needs are, what our experiences with language have been, and what our attitudes to ourselves and our language are. Underneath that vast range of differences, however, there are some more common factors that relate not so much to *what* we learn about language but to *how* we learn about language. Our challenge is to apply these factors to the individual needs and abilities of our students.

This chapter has been directed at the concern teachers have with students who show developmental differences in their language growth. While acknowledging these differences, we point out that they must always be considered within a context of use. Students who seem severely delayed still have considerable knowledge about language, and their development needs to proceed by extending this knowledge base. Traditionally, instruction for these students has involved removing language from meaningful contexts and focusing on specific aspects of language use. We would argue that these students, even more than the others, need to base their language growth on those factors that are fundamental to language development.

Mandie and Amy—the two girls whose language we quoted extensively in this chapter—confirmed for us what we increasingly understood as we wrote this book: We are all language users and learners who constantly strive to stretch our language to meet our needs and situations. As we do this throughout our lives, we develop a language that allows us to communicate with others, to think, and to imagine. Fortunately, from a curriculum point of view, "talk is cheap." When children have time to talk, they have access to a resource whose value in their lives is inestimable.

Some Useful Resources

Barnes, D. 1976. *From Communication to Curriculum.* New York: Penguin Books.

This classic book is a great help to teachers trying to implement an interactive model of teaching and learning in which students use their language as a means of making personal sense of school learning.

Barrs, M., S. Ellis, H. Tester, and A. Thomas. 1989. *The Primary Language Record: A Handbook for Teachers.* Portsmouth, N.H.: Heinemann.

A record-keeping tool for tracking children's language development that can guide and inform teachers who don't know a child, inform administrators of the child's work, and provide parents with information and assessment of the child's progress.

Cazden, C. B. 1988. *Classroom Discourse: The Language of Teaching and Learning.* Portsmouth, N.H.: Heinemann.

An interesting and useful review of recent research on classroom language.

Heath, S. B. 1983. *Ways with Words: Language, Life, and Work in Communities and Classrooms.* Cambridge: Cambridge University Press.

A readable and fascinating cross-cultural study of language and literacy development in the southeastern United States. An important book.

Language Arts. Published by the National Council of Teachers of English, Urbana, Illinois.

Language Arts regularly publishes useful articles by teachers and researchers on how to promote and use talk in the classroom.

Lindfors, J. W. 1980, 1987. *Children's Language and Learning.* Englewood Cliffs, N.J.: Prentice-Hall.

This book gives a readable overview of language theory and links it with classroom practice.

Toronto Board of Education. 1980. *Observing Children.* 155 College Street, Toronto, Ontario, Canada M5T 1P6.

This is a valuable guide to the informal observation of children's language from ages two to thirteen.

Tough, J. 1981. *A Place for Talk.* London: Ward Lock Educational.

Tough discusses the role of talk in the education of students with mild learning difficulties and considers how children might be helped to learn through the purposeful use of talk.

Wells, G. 1986. *The Meaning Makers: Children Learning Language and Using Language to Learn.* Portsmouth, N.H.: Heinemann.

This book draws on insights from a long-term study of language and literacy development to suggest ways teachers can help students grow as makers of meaning and creators of knowledge.

References

Apple, M. W. 1985. *Education and Power.* Boston: Ark Paperbooks.

Atwell, N. 1987. "Class-based writing research: Teachers learning from students." In *Reclaiming the Classroom: Teacher Research as an Agency for Change,* edited by D. Goswami and P. Stillman, 187–194. Portsmouth, N.H.: Boynton/Cook, Heinemann.

Barnes, D. 1976. *From Communication to Curriculum.* New York: Penguin.

Bartoli, J., and M. Botel. 1988. *Reading/Learning Disability: An Ecological Approach.* New York: Teachers College Press.

Bereiter, C., S. Engleman, J. Osborn, and P. A. Reidford. 1966. "An academically oriented pre-school for culturally deprived children." In *Pre-school Education Today,* edited by F. M. Hetchinger, 105–135. New York: Doubleday.

Berry, K. 1982. "Oral Learning of Grade Five Students in Small Group Discussion." Master's thesis, University of Alberta, Edmonton.

Bloom, L., and M. Lahey. 1978. *Language Development and Language Disorders.* New York: John Wiley and Sons.

Blount, B. G. 1977. "Ethnography and caretaker-child interaction." In *Talking to Children,* edited by C. E. Snow and C. A. Ferguson, 297–308. Cambridge: Cambridge University Press.

Britton, J. 1987. "A quiet form of research." In *Reclaiming the Classroom: Teacher Research as an Agency for Change,* edited by D. Goswami and P. Stillman, 13–19. Portsmouth, N.H.: Boynton/Cook, Heinemann.

Brown, R. 1973. *A First Language: The Early Stages.* Cambridge, Mass.: Harvard University Press.

139

————. 1977. Introduction. In *Talking to Children,* edited by C. E. Snow and C. A. Ferguson, 1–27. Cambridge: Cambridge University Press.

Calkins, L. M. 1986. *The Art of Teaching Writing.* Portsmouth, N.H.: Heinemann.

Cazden, C. B. 1970. "The neglected situation in child language research and education." In *Language and Poverty,* edited by F. Williams, 81–101. Chicago: Markham.

————. 1988. *Classroom Discourse: The Language of Teaching and Learning.* Portsmouth, N.H.: Heinemann.

Clarke, M. 1990. Telephone conversation with C. Dudley-Marling, 15 February.

Dillon, D., and D. Searle. 1981. "The role of language in one first-grade classroom." *Research in the Teaching of English* 15:311–328.

Donaldson, M. 1978. *Children's Minds.* Glasgow, Scotland: Fontana Press.

Dudley-Marling, C. 1990. *When School Is a Struggle.* Richmond Hill, Ont.: Scholastic-TAB.

Dudley-Marling, C., and D. Searle. 1988. "Enriching language-learning environments for students with learning disabilities." *Journal of Learning Disabilities* 21:140–143.

Edelsky, C. 1984. "The content of language arts software: A criticism." *Computers, Reading, and Language Arts* 1:8–11.

Elliot, A. 1991. "An Investigation of the School-based Language Use of a Selected Group of Primary Students Identified as Language Disordered." Master's thesis, Faculty of Education, York University, Toronto.

Good, T. C. 1980. "Classroom expectations: Teacher-pupil interactions." In *The Social Psychology of School Learning,* edited by J. H. McMillan, 79–122. New York: Academic Press.

Hansen, J. 1987. *When Writers Read.* Portsmouth, New Hampshire: Heinemann.

Hassler, D. M. 1979. *A Successful Transplant of Wait-time and Questioning Strategies to Children's Oral Language Behaviors.* Washington, D.C.: American University. (ERIC Document Reproduction Service No. ED 205 951.)

Heath, S. B. 1985. *Ways with Words: Language, Life, and Work in Communities and Classrooms.* Cambridge: Cambridge University Press.

Holt, J. 1982. *How Children Fail.* 2nd ed. New York: Delacorte Press/Seymour Lawrence.

Honea, J. M., Jr. 1982. "Wait-time as an instructional variable: An influence on teacher and student." *Clearing House* 56:167–170.

Jaggar, A. 1989. "Teachers as learners: Implications for staff development." In *Teachers and Research,* edited by G. S. Pinnell and M. L. Matlin, 66–80. Newark, Del.: International Reading Association.

Jones, P. 1988. *Lipservice: The Story of Talk in Schools.* Philadelphia, Pa.: Open University Press.

Labov, W. 1972. *Language of the Inner City.* Philadelphia, Pa.: University of Pennsylvania Press.

Lehr, F. 1984. "Student-teacher communication." *Language Arts,* 61:200–203.

Lindfors, J. W. 1980. *Children's Language and Learning.* Englewood Cliffs, N.J.: Prentice-Hall.

Loughlin, C. E., and M. D. Martin. 1987. *Supporting Literacy: Developing Effective Learning Environments.* New York: Teachers College Press.

Marland, D. 1977. *Language Across the Curriculum.* London: Heinemann.

Martin, N. 1976. Tutorial with Dennis Searle. University of London, England.

Mattioli, J. 1990. "One Language Delayed Child's Use of Language in Different Settings with Different Conversational Participants." Unpublished paper, Faculty of Education, York University, Toronto.

Mehan, H. 1979. *Learning Lessons.* Cambridge, Mass.: Harvard University Press.

Michaels, S. 1981. "Sharing time: Children's narrative style and differential access to literacy." *Language in Society* 10:423–442.

Michaels, S., and M. Foster. 1985. "Peer-peer learning: Evidence from a student-run sharing time." In *Observing the Language Learner,* edited by A. Jaggar and M. T. Smith-Burke, 143–158. Newark, Del.: International Reading Association.

Milz, V. E. 1989. "Comments from a teacher researcher." In *Teachers and Research,* edited by G. S. Pinnell and M. L. Matlin, 25–28. Newark, Del.: International Reading Association.

Newton, J. 1988. "Teachers' language in classroom learning." In *Teacher as Researcher,* edited by M. Chorny, 33–56. Calgary, Alberta: Language in the Classroom Project, University of Calgary.

Odell, L. 1989. "Planning classroom research." In *Reclaiming the Classroom: Teacher Research as an Agency for Change,* edited by D. Goswami and P. Stillman, 128–160. Portsmouth, N.H.: Boynton/Cook, Heinemann.

Poplin, M. S. 1988. "The reductionist fallacy in learning disabilities: Replicating the past by reducing the present." *Journal of Learning Disabilities* 21:389–400.

Rosen, C., and H. Rosen. 1973. *The Language of Primary School Children.* Baltimore, Md.: Penguin.

Searle, D. 1984. "Scaffolding: Who's building whose building?" *Language Arts* 61:480–483.
———. 1988. "Language: A tool for learning." In *Teacher as Researcher,* edited by M. Chorny, 5–32. Calgary, Alberta: Language in the Classroom Project, University of Calgary.
Smith, F. 1986. *Insult to Intelligence: The Bureaucratic Invasion of Our Classrooms.* New York: Arbor Press.
Staab, C. F. 1982. "Classroom practice for facilitating oral language: Improving semantic and syntactic cueing systems." *Reading Improvement* 19:250–256.
Strickland, D., R. M. Dillon, L. Funkhouser, M. Glick, and C. Rogers. 1989. "Research currents: Classroom dialogue during literature response groups." *Language Arts* 66:192–200.

Tough, J. 1976. *Listening to Children Talking: A Guide to the Appraisal of Children's Use of Language.* London: Ward Lock Educational.
———. 1981. *A Place for Talk.* London: Ward Lock Educational.

Vgotsky, L. S. 1986. *Thought and Language.* Cambridge: MIT Press.

Ward, M. C. 1971. *Them Children: A Study of Language Learning.* New York: Holt, Rinehart, and Winston.

Index